Embedding Culture into Video Games and Game Design

This book will help game designers and those interested in games thoughtfully embed culture into video games and the game design process.

This book raises the issue of how some cultures and communities are misrepresented in various video games. In response to this problem, designers can bring cultural considerations and practices into the centre focus of the game design process. The book advocates that designers put different measures in place to better prevent misrepresentations and engage with deeper understandings of culture to build culturally richer and more meaningful game worlds. The book uses the Torres Strait Virtual Reality project as a primary example, in addition to other game projects, to explore cultural representation in game design. Torres Strait culture is also explored and discussed more broadly throughout the book. No prior knowledge of culture studies is needed, and the book deals with higher level game design with little reference to the technical elements of game development.

This unique and timely book will appeal to those interested in the implications of cultural depictions in video games and opportunities to generate deeper cultural representations through the game design process.

Rhett Loban is a Lecturer in the School of Education at Macquarie University. His research interests include culture, game-based learning and virtual reality.

Embedding Culture into Video Games and Game Design

The Palm, the Dogai and the Tombstone

Rhett Loban

CRC Press
Taylor & Francis Group
Boca Raton London New York

CRC Press is an imprint of the
Taylor & Francis Group, an **informa** business

A CHAPMAN & HALL BOOK

Designed cover image: The Palm, the Dogai and the Tombstone [Painting]. Illustration by Xia Hua.

First edition published 2024
by CRC Press
2385 NW Executive Center Drive, Suite 320, Boca Raton FL 33431

and by CRC Press
4 Park Square, Milton Park, Abingdon, Oxon, OX14 4RN

CRC Press is an imprint of Taylor & Francis Group, LLC

Library of Congress Cataloging-in-Publication Data
Names: Loban, Rhett, author.
Title: Embedding culture into video games and game design : the palm, the Dogai and the tombstone / Rhett Loban.
Description: Boca Raton : CRC Press, 2024. | Includes bibliographical references and index.
Identifiers: LCCN 2023010956 (print) | LCCN 2023010957 (ebook) | ISBN 9781032232164 (hardback) | ISBN 9781032232195 (paperback) | ISBN 9781003276289 (ebook)
Subjects: LCSH: Video games--Social aspects. | Video games--Design. | Torres Strait Islanders--Social life and customs. | Torres Strait--In mass media.
Classification: LCC GV1469.34.S52 L64 2024 (print) | LCC GV1469.34.S52 (ebook) | DDC 794.8/3--dc23/eng/20230406
LC record available at https://lccn.loc.gov/2023010956
LC ebook record available at https://lccn.loc.gov/2023010957

ISBN: 978-1-032-23216-4 (hbk)
ISBN: 978-1-032-23219-5 (pbk)
ISBN: 978-1-003-27628-9 (ebk)

DOI: 10.1201/9781003276289

Typeset in Times
by KnowledgeWorks Global Ltd.

Contents

Acknowledgements

I have in part written this book for my family, particularly my son Finn, so he can better understand his culture and family history. I am very thankful to my immediate family members, including my mother, sisters and especially my father, Mr. Gehamat Loban, who was deeply involved in the Torres Strait Virtual Reality (TSVR) project that this book discusses. Not only did he provide his cultural expertise and knowledge to the project, but he also provided his artistic and educational expertise through his sketches and narration for TSVR. I would also like to thank my wife Chen and her parents for their support of the project and the writing of this book. I am indebted to my immediate and extended families for their help and for permissions to use information and photographs in the book. I would like to express gratitude to the Torres Strait Islander community, which provided feedback and supported the project. The wider Indigenous and Australian communities also provided input into and support for TSVR, to whom I am grateful.

I would like to acknowledge and thank the two student developers, Mr. Junhao Shentu and Mr. Jing Xu, for their assistance in building TSVR and bringing the world to life. I am deeply grateful to the University of New South Wales (UNSW) that funded the project, as well as the support from the project managers, including Dr. Courtenay Atwell (and her husband Chris), Mr. Ricardo Thomson and Mr. Luis Carlos Dominguez. I am thankful to the unit convenors who supported the project, worked with us and allowed us to implement TSVR in their university units.I am also indebted to Dr. Xia Hua for creating the front cover and other paintings for the book.

I would like to extend my gratitude to the reviewers who provided feedback and reviewed the book, including Associate Professor Dorothy DeWitt, Associate Professor Neil Harrison and Dr. Elizabeth LaPensée. I am indebted to Dr. John Ehrich and Professor Rauno Parrila for their general feedback on the book. I would also like to thank Dr. Aunty Kaye Price AM, Professor Dorottya Fabian, Mr. Liam Ridgeway and Mr. Geoff Guymer and the rest of the team at CSIRO for their support through the CSIRO Indigenous STEM Awards. I would like to thank the many friends, including Mr. Jason Chan, who have supported me and the project through the years. There are many colleagues at both UNSW and Macquarie University who have been highly supportive of the project, and I am grateful to them. I am also thankful for the many others who have helped the project and myself on this journey.

Figure 0.1 The Palm, the Dogai and the Tombstone [painting]. Illustration by Xia Hua.

Preface

Acknowledgement of country

I would like to acknowledge the Wangal clan and the Wattamattagal clan, who are traditional custodians of the lands on which I live, work and wrote this book. I wish to pay respects to Elders past, present and emerging.

Indigenous Australian Concept – Country or Place/Island

While definitions of Country or Place/Island will vary between different communities, Country and Place/Island can be concepts used by Indigenous people in Australia to describe the land or waters they belong to and where they often live. However, this connection is also a cultural and spiritual connection to the land or waters. For example, community stories and knowledge are intimately connected and often understood in relation to the very landscape, sea or sky itself. Country tends to be used by Aboriginal people, while Place or Island tends to be used by Torres Strait Islander people. However, these terms may vary, and other words could be used from community to community.

Who am I?

I would like to introduce myself and my cultural background, so you understand my perspective and who I am. My name is Rhett Loban, and I was born in Brisbane, Australia, on the land of the Turrbal people (though I am not a part of this tribe). My father is from Waiben (or Thursday Island) in the Torres Straits with further connections to Mabuyag and Boigu. My mother is from Dundee, Scotland. I was raised in both a Torres Strait and a Scottish household in Australia. However, for the purpose of this book and to discuss the game for which I led the development, I am mostly drawing upon the teachings from my father's family and culture, which I learned growing up, as well as my own experience with the Torres Straits. The way I have been raised has strongly shaped my view on culture and how I approached the game design process outlined in this book.

What is the central problem and response posed in this book?

This book raises the problem of how some cultures and communities are misrepresented, poorly portrayed, or not represented at all within video games. Sometimes the representations in these video games are made by game designers and not from the cultures that are being depicted in-game. While some in-game misrepresentations are often unintentional and even with good intentions, these cultural in-game depictions are representing cultures where the designer may have limited or no knowledge of and experience with the culture or community. Part of the issue here is that in some cases the designers' imaginings and even unconscious biases can shape how different cultures are depicted in-game, which produces misrepresentations of the culture. However, another more crucial part of the issue for game designers is that they may be missing out on opportunities to engage with and represent deeper and richer aspects of culture to build much more complex, vibrant and engaging game worlds. That is more than just building a culturally sound game; there are opportunities to represent unique and meaningful cultural perspectives and worldviews.

In response to this problem, designers can bring cultural considerations and practices into the centre focus of the game design process. Designers can put different measures in place to better prevent misrepresentations and engage with deeper understandings of culture to build game worlds. The book emphasises community participation, immersion in the culture and rigorous research of the culture to help thoughtfully engage and integrate culture into the design process and video game output. Through this process, designers can also form respectful and reciprocal relationships with the community being represented in-game. The book explores the game design process of Torres Strait Virtual Reality (TSVR) as an example of how one might thoughtfully integrate cultural practices and considerations into game design. TSVR is a virtual reality video game designed around the Torres Strait Tombstone Opening Ceremony (also known as a Tombstone Unveiling). Torres Strait culture is also explored and discussed more broadly throughout the book.

While the book will primarily use the TSVR project to discuss game design, it will also refer to other game design examples to explore the challenges, benefits and processes associated with embedding culture into games. This book draws upon the Torres Strait concepts of the cultural palm tree and the Dogai (a spirit) to illustrate the continuum from deeper cultural representations to surface-level representations in-game. In this book, I will argue that greater involvement of people from the culture depicted in-game throughout the game design will typically yield deeper and more genuine cultural representations in-game. Community participation can be further supported by the cultural immersion of the designer and rigorous research of the culture and community. In contrast, game design approaches without thoughtful consideration of the culture will likely lead to cultural depictions that may appear sound but are not representative of deep understandings of the culture. In essence, I believe we are thinking about ways to tell stories through the medium and, for me, this process begins with getting the story and content right in the first place in order to build culturally deeper worlds and representations.

Who might find this book useful?

This book is aimed at helping those working with games to consider how culture and community might be thoughtfully embedded into games and their design process. While this book may be read by game designers and those involved in the video game industry, I also anticipate it could be read by those creating other kinds of digital media more generally. I believe that the approach to embedding culture into games described in this book can also be loosely applied to the creation of other kinds of digital media. The book has been strongly informed by cultural and educational research. Therefore, the issues and recommendations in this book may also be applicable to problems around the representation of cultures and communities we encounter in education and teaching. Those studying digital humanities, information technology and computing more broadly may also find this book informative. No prior knowledge of cultural or educational studies is needed, and the book mostly deals with higher level game design with only some reference to the technical elements of broader game development.

This book is also about Torres Strait Islander culture, with TSVR itself being a cultural representation of the Torres Straits. Therefore, those interested in learning about Torres Strait Islander culture and Indigenous Australia more broadly may find this book useful. The book also has a chapter on the Torres Straits, with a focus on the place and family history to provide a foundational understanding of the Torres Strait community. I have interwoven cultural knowledge and stories throughout the book. For example, you will find my father, who has been involved in many Tombstone Openings, discussing the process and practices around the Tombstone Opening in the book's prologue, interludes and epilogue. There are also Torres Strait stories and knowledge dispersed and discussed throughout the book, which can be found in many of the panels with blue text. I feel communicating aspects of Torres Strait culture is important, so that you as the reader have a greater sense of my culture which I have embedded into TSVR and its design processes.

How to use this book?

In total, this book is part informational about Torres Strait culture and community, part theoretical in the exploration of representations of cultures and communities within video games and game design and part practice in how culture and community are integrated into and affect the game design process. This book is organised into chapters that cover different topics, but holistically, it is divided into sections that cover the theory of representation, game design practice and information about the Torres Straits for greater context about the game. The discussion of the theory is primarily in Chapters 1, 3 and 7. Discussion of game design practice is mainly in Chapters 4–7. Information about the Torres Straits is largely in Chapters 2–4 as well as the prologue, interludes, epilogue and many of the blue panels throughout the book. However, some blue panels provide more information on other important and connected concepts related to the book. You can target and use specific chapters based on your interests. The breakdown of the chapters is as follows:

- Chapter 1 (a theory chapter) introduces the book and outlines the challenges surrounding representations of cultures in video games. The book introduces the definition of culture and presents the book's intent of exploring and responding to the issues of cultural representation in video games. The chapter considers the theoretical origin and basis of the issues around cultural representations in video games while drawing on examples to further illustrate the issues. The chapter suggests game design centred around meaningful engagement with culture and community as a response to cultural misrepresentations and to create deeper cultural representations in-game. Read this chapter for an introduction to the book and to understand the basic issues about cultural representations in media, including video games.
- Chapter 2 (an information chapter) provides a brief contextual overview of the Torres Straits with a focus on the geography and a brief history of the Torres Strait community from the perspective of the author's family. The chapter offers guidance on the type of foundational understanding that designers may need to develop for their own game design projects. This chapter provides a baseline understanding of the islands, region and languages of the Torres Straits and more recent Torres Strait Islander history, including the pearling industry, contributions to the railways, national service and community development. Read this chapter to familiarise yourself with the Torres Straits, the Torres Strait Islander community and the context of the discussion of TSVR.
- Chapter 3 (an information and theory chapter) discusses the theoretical framework for understanding and addressing the issue of cultural representation in video games. Building on academic literature around surface culture, deep culture and the simulacrum, this chapter proposes the Torres Strait concepts of the cultural palm and the Dogai as frameworks for understanding cultural representations in games. The palm is representative of a culture that can shift over time, but ultimately comes from a deep place. In contrast, the Dogai is representative of cultural depictions that might appear to be from the culture but are only surface-level portrayals and are recognised by the community as shallow representations. Read this chapter to understand the theoretical framework around surface- and deeper-level cultural representations.
- Chapter 4 (an information and practice chapter) details the game design processes and challenges encountered while attempting to centre culture in the development of TSVR. The chapter explores different aspects of the design process of TSVR and how cultural considerations and practices were incorporated into the game design and decision-making process. This chapter is a more detailed and practical exploration of how culture was brought into the TSVR design process, including in the project team, the story, in-game depictions, utilised assets and the implementation of TSVR. Read this chapter for a detailed breakdown of the different ways culture was represented in TSVR and applied through the design process.

- Chapter 5 (a practice chapter) examines different processes for involving the community in the game design process – from embedding community members into the game design team to engaging knowledge holders through to including the community in the playtest and quality assurance processes. This chapter has practical recommendations about how to involve and engage the community throughout the game design process. The chapter also discusses how to make contact with the community and raise awareness about the differing organisational structures between some organisations (e.g., corporations) and some community organisations. Some community organisations can be intertwined with cultural and kinship groups and relationships, and, therefore, such organisations are key to engaging communities. Read this chapter for suggestions about approaching, involving and integrating community into the game's design.
- Chapter 6 (a practice chapter) discusses how cultural immersion and rigorous research can be used to support the design process. The chapter discusses the ethics of including culture in-game. Designers who participate in cultural immersion can gain a better understanding of culture within the context of a community and can begin reciprocal relationships with the community. Designers can also engage in rigorous research to better locate and utilise more appropriate materials to use in designing game worlds. Designers should also consider the ethics of how to best represent culture in-game and its impact on other aspects of the project such as monetisation. This chapter details different approaches from the literature on cultural immersion as well as practical steps for assessing the appropriateness of different resources for use in game design. Read this chapter to understand cultural immersion, how to choose materials for building your game world and the ethics of cultural representations in games.
- Chapter 7 (a theory and practice chapter) summarises the book while also outlining the main points, key suggestions, the book's limitations and possible future directions of the issue of cultural representation in games. This chapter discusses the cultural lens and self-reflection as well as the benefits of triangulation. The chapter also highlights the need for a thoughtful engagement with culture in the game design process and finding the balance in the overall project and game design approach. The chapter also discusses the process over outcome approach and how designers could integrate culture into games and game design with confidence. Read this chapter for a summary and the key messages and suggestions from the book.

Prologue

The recent passing of a relative or community member

Remarks from Gehamat Loban

Figure P.1 A typical setting for the 7-day, 40-day and 100-day gatherings. A white cloth sheet laid over a woven island palm mat with servings of fruit, cake and tea for the attendees [photograph]. Year: Circa 1963–1964.

In Torres Strait customs, we often follow a process and practice of mourning the deceased. This process and practice will vary between families as Torres Strait culture is highly diverse with many intermarriages between islander people and other communities brought to the islands. Islanders embrace the culture of their spouses, but the spouses also take on islander culture. Thus, customs can vary from family to family depending on the background of the Torres Strait Islander person. When an Islander person with Muslim Malay background passes away, there is a process to mourn and pay respect to the deceased. The mourning ends with the Tombstone Opening, which is the largest feast and gathering of family and community.

DOI: 10.1201/9781003276289-1

However, there are smaller 7-day, 40-day and 100-day gatherings and other protocols to follow before the Tombstone Opening (see Figure P.1 for a typical smaller gathering arrangement).

Soon after the passing, people from the community visit to pay their respects and offer their condolences to the family of the deceased with the funeral soon to follow. However, before the funeral, as relatives or close persons within the community, we wash the deceased and wrap them in a white calico sheet. This practice may have been the same for females washing their own gender. All members of the family and close community members would take any sheeting left over and tear strips from the white cloth. We then tie a strip around our wrist, which we have to keep on for up to 100 days or until it falls off. However, we would not remove it before then. Typically occurring within or close to the 7 days, the funeral follows with a gathering of family and close community members. In addition, during and up until the 40-day gathering, we do not play any music or have celebrations after the death. For the 7-day, 40-day and 100-day gatherings, family members, friends and close community members come together to show their respect for the deceased. Decisions about the gatherings and protocols are made by the family of the deceased.

At each of the 7-day, 40-day and 100-day gatherings, there was a typical process that we undertook as children and grandsons. We would go with our Datos (grandfathers) to the gatherings with all the other Malay Muslim men. Again, there may have been other processes for women to which we were not privy. We begin the ceremony by sitting cross-legged on a white sheet on the floor, waiting for the Datos to start the event. The most senior Datos would lead and start the prayer with others joining in. Incenses were lit for the gathering, and the adults often placed or tied a cloth over their heads during the ceremony. During this smaller gathering between us and the Datos, lighter foods such as fruit, cake and tea are served. After we finish the prayer, coins are gathered from attendees and are given to us as the attending grandsons. Once this smaller ceremony has finalised, we would join a larger gathering involving the rest of the attendees. We all join together for makan (eating) with set tables and cooked meals. These actions were in the spirit of sharing with the community and performing good deeds during the mourning period for the deceased. After the 7-day, 40-day and 100-day gatherings for mourning the deceased, the next part of our mourning process continues with preparing for the Tombstone Opening.

1 Cultural representations in video games

Located in Far North Queensland in Australia and beyond Cape York, the Torres Strait Islands have a local ceremony dedicated to a person who has passed away. This ceremony is the Tombstone Opening. The Tombstone Opening indicates the end of a mourning period for the deceased and is central to island custom (Beckett, 1990). It is an anchor in island society and brings families from other islands and mainland Australia to plan, prepare and present the grave (Smith & Bird, 2000). The event also involves feasting, dancing, singing and arrangements for the guests (Singe, 1979). Although originating as a Muslim Malay tradition from my perspective, today the Tombstone Opening combines Islamic and Christian burial practices with Islander artefacts and traditions (Elu, 2004). Cultural and religious synchronisations have blended different understandings of the world and, in some instances, ended inter-island conflicts in the Torres Straits.

The Tombstone Opening formed the foundation for the storyline of Torres Strait Virtual Reality (TSVR). TSVR is a virtual reality (VR) game created to communicate Torres Strait Islander culture and knowledge through an immersive and interactive medium. While the digital representation of the Tombstone Opening might be simple to technically recreate in a gaming environment, the process of a thoughtful and genuine cultural representation requires deeper consideration and understanding of the process and protocols involved in the event. Here, an appreciation of the context of the event and greater insight into Torres Strait culture itself are required. This emphasis on culture was the central focus of the TSVR game design and the process through which TSVR was developed.

Similarly, a central focus of this book is culture and how it is represented in games through the game design and development process. There are various definitions of culture; however, my father, who is a Torres Strait Elder and an educator himself for over 20 years, defines culture as a way of life. Culture is being, knowing, thinking and doing for him, and these realities and actions are evident in various cultural practices, including storytelling, hunting, fishing, art, gardening, cooking, dancing, singing and many other cultural customs. These activities are all cultural practices, but they also guide how one decides to live their life. From the moment you wake up with your bed facing the rising sun to dinner at night where we would sit down as a family to eat Torres Strait food, culture is practiced all the time, consciously and

DOI: 10.1201/9781003276289-2

unconsciously. This definition is similar to many academic definitions such as Gallagher et al. (2019) who see culture as a way of life from a Māori cultural context, where a community will live by certain ideals such as the importance of building relationships. Myers (1987) defines culture as the "total way of life of a people" (p. 72) in her exploration of culture in contemporary life. Williams (1983) sees culture in several ways with reference to high culture, but more pertinently, Williams sees culture as a particular way of life for a people, group or time period. Further to this, Williams also sees culture as including cultural objects such as music, literature and various forms of art. Cultural objects could be seen as the product or output of a particular way of life of a group, and can be deeply connected to that way of life. These understandings of culture and definitions of culture focus on culture as a way of life and how those from a particular culture can have cultural experiences as everyday experiences and live by ideals that inform their worldview.

Torres Strait terminology – respected community and familial titles

In the Torres Straits, we use different titles to refer to knowledge holders and respected community members. These titles also signify relationships between community members. Many of these terms originate from Indonesia and the broader Malay Archipelago. See a list and explanation of titles in the following:

- Dato is a grandfather, but also refers to a very senior and respected community or family member.
- Puman refers to a senior and respected community or family member but not as senior as Dato.
- Nene is a grandmother, but also refers to a very senior and respected community or family member.
- Abung and Kaka refer to the eldest brother and sister, respectively, but are also used as titles of respect and position within family structures.
- Bebe and Pache refer to aunt and uncle, respectively, but are also used as titles of respect and position within family structures.
- Elder is also used within the community, but has only been recently introduced as a contemporary title. Depending on the circumstance, Dato, Nene and Elder can be used interchangeably.

From a game studies perspective, Penix-Tadsen (2016) sees culture as having a double meaning in his book *Cultural Code*. He views culture as a synonym for human society (e.g. practices of a community), but within the game's culture it is also representative of symbols, the environment and narratives that embody a specific community. Similarly, in the approach of my book, cultural practices in conjunction with game design can be used to help inform the cultural representations within the game. Hutchinson (2019), in her book *Japanese Culture through Videogames*, has multiple definitions for cultures; however, she ultimately sees culture as being bound up in identity, a sense of who the community is and how that community thinks and acts. This definition also emphasises identity and a community's thoughts and actions, all of which can be shaped by a way of life and experiences that can be shared by the community.

Culture is also inherent in the idea of cultural heritage, which is defined as "the legacy that we receive from the past, experience in the present, and transmit to future generations" (Pelegrini, 2008, p. 2215). Generally, cultural heritage could be "sites, things, and practices a society regards as old, important, and worthy of conservation" (Brumann, 2015, p. 414). In this way, cultural heritage can be divided into two categories, physical artefacts and intangible attributes, both of which can be inherited from previous generations and are seen as helping characterise and identify the distinctiveness of a society (Willis, 2014, p. 147). In a larger list, cultural heritage can include:

> cultures, customs, beliefs, rites, rituals, ceremonies, indigenous knowledge, social customs and traditions, arts, crafts, music, political and ideological beliefs that influence culture and behavior, history, practices concerning the natural environment, religious and scientific traditions, language, sports, food and drink, calendars, traditional clothing, cybercultures in the digital world, and emerging new cultures which will become the heritage of the future (Baker, 2013, p. 121).

Aspects of cultural heritage seem to interlink with the notion of tangible objects and intangible thoughts and practices that can be passed from one generation to the next. Here, cultural heritage can come in various forms and is regarded as important by that community and can be transferable between generations.

Clearly, there are different approaches as to how culture is defined. Seemingly, culture connects people through shared practices, representations of wider society, identity and so on, which are all relevant to the culture in which one lives. Indeed, throughout each of the definitions, there is a reference to how life is lived and the context in which that person lives. Some terms such as cultural heritage imply that tangible objects and intangible thoughts and practices are passed between generations. For example, transmission can occur through storytelling such as how the story of the Dogai is told, or could it occur through practice such as how the process of mourning and the Tombstone Opening is passed on to next generations. It should also be noted that these aspects of culture can evolve between generations. Thus, for the purposes of this book, I consider culture as a way of life shared by a group of people that can be passed on and evolve between generations. This understanding of culture heavily emphasises experience as a way culture is carried out in practice and how it might be passed on to following generations. This definition is not to say all people from the same community will all have the same experiences, but that some aspects will likely be shared, hence a shared culture.

Culture can also be reflected in the outputs from a community, for example, in the form of video games.

> ### Torres Strait story – the Dogai
>
> The Dogai is a female spirit who features in many Torres Strait stories often as the antagonist. She holds many powers such as shapeshifting, commanding nature and reattaching severed body parts. Two Dogais feature in the TSVR. The Dogai will be discussed in detail further in the book.

Culture and video games

Games and their design and development are the other central aspects of this book. In this book, games are defined as a "form of play with goals and structure" (Maroney, 2001). For a video game or a digital game, this process is mediated by a PC or an electronic gaming system. However, when culture is introduced to a game, does the game then become a cultural game, such as a Japanese video game? What makes a particular game, a game from a given culture? Hutchinson (2019) defines a Japanese game as a game that has been developed by a studio in Japan or with their head office located in Japan. This definition is sound for dominant cultures that are intertwined with the nation state and have the capacity to represent their own culture independently, at least to some extent. However, from the perspective of colonised Indigenous nations, LaPensée et al. (2022) view games where Indigenous people have leading roles in the game's development as sovereign games. These sovereign games are spaces for Indigenous representations and are expressions of their own culture. Through sovereign games, Indigenous people can reclaim their self-determination within a digital space. Thus, a cultural game (e.g. a Japanese game or a sovereign game for an Indigenous community) is a game developed by an individual or an organisation from a culture, particularly where that culture is represented in-game.

In researching Japanese cultural games, Hutchinson (2019) suggests that "at the most basic level, Japanese games offer us a Japanese view of the world" (p. 256). Hutchinson (2019) sees the relationship between a Japanese video game and Japan as a relationship between the game and its context. This relationship between the game's representation and its cultural context is important in understanding the game and how the developers see their own culture. The community's view of their own culture can vary from person to person, which can then be reflected in a game and the design of that game. Indeed, there is no specific or essentialised idea or theme that defines a game from a community. Nonetheless, these cultural games are often how that community sees the world and even how they see themselves (Hutchinson, 2019).

As mentioned, some cultures and communities can represent and speak for themselves through their games to some degree such as the Japanese nation via their games industry. However, this self-representation is not true for all games or for all cultures, with some cultures often being misrepresented by outsiders of that culture. These misrepresentations, especially by those not a part of the culture being depicted, are not always intentionally malicious, yet they seem to occur frequently enough within the gaming industry that the misrepresented communities are speaking out against such depictions. The problem of misrepresentation has been present long before the arrival of video games and has been an issue grappled with in other media and literature.

The theories of cultural representation and depictions in research and literature

An important theorist in the discussion of cultural misrepresentation in texts and media is Edward Said, who wrote the book *Orientalism* (1978). In essence, Orientalism can be seen as the exaggerated and biased ways in which Western nations often view outside countries and peoples (Said, 1978). Said specifically examines how Western nations, especially Britain, France and the United States of America, viewed non-Western nations and communities. In his book, Said discusses the Middle East, or what is often thought of as part of the Orient. Through the colonisation of non-Western nations by Western nations, the West came to view Middle Eastern people in certain and often exaggerated ways. This view was typically only from their own perspective, without any in-depth understanding of the people they colonised. The colonisation process was not only the invasion and subjugation of non-Western nations and peoples, but also how colonialists conceived and produced biased views and knowledge of the non-Western world even unintentionally. Western colonisation and military expansion went hand in hand with intellectual and academic endeavours to produce biased views and knowledge of the people the Western nations subjugated.

According to Said (1978), historical Western literature and other works, for example, works by Arthur Balfour, Lord Cromer (Evelyn Baring) and Gustave Flaubert, depicted societies and people in the Middle East in highly prejudiced and stereotypical ways from irrational and depraved to exotic and sensual. In essence, non-Western societies were painted as fundamentally different from Western societies (Said, 1978). In colonist literature and art, people from the Middle East were depicted as snake charmers, courtesans and despots (Gérôme, 1866, 1879; Lowe, 2018; Said, 1978). These exoticised and often negative views became central to the way these communities were depicted in various literatures and art by Western nations.

The Western authors' and artists' limited understandings and even prejudices are presented as an empirical truth in literary, artistic or research outputs often without the perspective of those being studied or observed (Said, 1978). Certainly, scholars were in contact with these cultures and communities. However, it was the observer's perceptions and biases from positions of power, as temporary visitors and as outsiders of the community that influenced what and how they saw the culture and its people. Pertinently, these Orientalist lens of the non-Western world has continued long after freedom was gained by some colonised nations and Orientalist perspectives still influence how the Western world conceives the non-Western world and even how non-Western nations see themselves (Said, 1978). Orientalist depictions in our media have continued into our contemporary context, and even initial experiences with these communities through such media can affect how we see communities.

Exposure to exaggerated and biased representations in the media can have continued knock-on effects on the way viewers perceive a culture or community, even within today's context. First encounters can predispose a person to a view of a culture, even if that experience is through a piece of media. For example, if you play a game that depicts a community in a certain way, a picture is already being painted in the mind of the player about this community. This occurs even without the player ever encountering anyone from the represented culture. Then, if we were to meet someone from that culture or even go to the homeland of this community, we would form new understandings about this culture. However, these understandings are compared to our initial exposure and, as a consequence, we try to find patterns and similarities to reconcile what we have seen in our first exposure. In this way, it does not matter whether the culture or community matches what was depicted in our first exposure, we are consciously or subconsciously attempting to match expectations with our initial exposure to the culture in the game. Here, we are already formulating a confirmation bias at the back of our minds, even before we encounter a community face-to-face.

Brayboy et al. (2012) also discuss similar issues around representations in their work and highlight how "research" is considered a dirty word in many Indigenous communities. In the past, Indigenous people have been subjected to low ethical standards of research and often seen in highly clinical ways. Sometimes these researched communities were studied as if they were a part of the flora and fauna. These views and approaches to different communities are reproduced through the research and result in a one-sided and typically outsider conceptualisation of that community. In some past approaches to research with Indigenous communities, the interests of the researcher or funder of the research have been the primary focus and not necessarily the interests of people from the community.

In a global context, the academic endeavours and studies in various communities around the world then feed into a wider global monopoly on academic thought controlled by Western nations. Connell (2018) draws attention to how biases in science and knowledge were also centred on and developed by the Western world. Connell (2018) discusses how this issue is not so much an issue of Western science, but rather what she calls imperial science. Information and intellectual materials were passed from the colonised nations or the peripheries to the nation's metropole or imperial centre, where all the information and materials were processed and analysed from Western perspectives. In this case, the colonised world served as a source of raw data, but this data was aggregated and analysed in Western metropoles and then sent back to the peripheries. This process removed Indigenous knowledge and information from their original context and understanding, and instead interpreted it from a Western perspective. This monopoly on knowledge around the globe helped promote the research and knowledge system of the West as the intellectual authority, superior scholarly method and all-encompassing and universal science. The monopoly on how information from around the globe is processed and controlled is another example of how a particular perspective of the world is promoted while others are not.

The crux of the issue is that Western perspectives have shaped and continue to strongly shape historical and current literature, art and research with the media misrepresenting different cultures and communities. Authors, artists and researchers have not necessarily sought the views of those being represented. Though some of the researchers and authors may be living or spending time in the depicted communities, we do not necessarily hear from the communities themselves and ask how they see themselves. This issue is not to say that none of this literature, art or research has generated any valuable understanding or was not well intentioned. However, the typical approach and power imbalance meant that the story was primarily told from one perspective and that perspective may often have had limited knowledge and understandings of the culture and community. These one-sided understandings are not necessarily a true reflection of the culture or the communities and especially not how these communities see themselves. The practical implication of this approach is that we can form exaggerated, unfair and sometimes false views of different cultures and communities without even having met them or only having engaged with them in typically superficial ways. The biased views can thus manifest themselves in the way we produce media, including in video games.

Misrepresented cultural depictions in video games

Cultural representations in video games are commonplace and help build game worlds by filling them with life, characters and cultural settings. However, many non-Western cultures, especially Indigenous cultures around the world, are often misrepresented and sometimes depicted offensively in games. A blatant video game example of a problematic representation by a developer is the *Survival Island 3 – Australia* game (NIL Entertainment, 2015), where players were encouraged to fight and kill Aboriginal non-playable characters in-game (Connaughton, 2016). A petition criticising the game stated that the promotion of the game claimed that players would "Meet real aboriginals" and that players would "have to fight with aboriginals" (N A, 2016). An in-game screenshot advertising the game also cautions players to "beware of Aborigines" (ABC News, 2016). Such depictions play into historical tropes representing Aboriginal Australian people as vicious and hostile, and as just a part of the flora and fauna that the player needs to tame or pacify in-game. A report indicated that the developer was based in Siberia and had little understanding of Indigenous Australian cultures (Connaughton, 2016). The game has been removed from the Apple and Google online stores. This example was a relatively less known developer creating a small video game. However, larger game companies with global reach can also perpetuate a limited or biased understanding of other cultures.

Representations in the *Mortal Kombat* game series such as in *Mortal Kombat 3* (Midway, 1995) feed into the mystic and savage Native American trope through their depiction of the playable character Nightwolf who uses an array of animal spirit powers to fight other combatants (Longboat, 2019; Printup, 2019). This depiction contributes to Native American stereotypes and there is criticism that there seems to be little attempt to thoughtfully redesign or retire the character even with rejections of the representation by the Native American community (Printup, 2019). Similarly, the Cree community expressed disappointment at portrayal of Cree nation leader Pîhtokahanapiwiyin (also known as Poundmaker) in *Civilisation VI* (Campbell, 2018; Firaxis Games, 2016). Milton Tootoosis, a Cree headman, expressed concerns that the Cree depiction in-game perpetuates the myth of First Nations being conquerors (Campbell, 2018). This example is particularly offensive to the Cree community who tried to broker peaceful negotiations between Canadian authorities and the Cree community. Tootoosis was disappointed that 2K Games (the game's developers) had not approached any Cree representatives during development. In these examples, large corporations with significant pools of resources are also responsible for misrepresentations that arguably have greater global reach and influence.

In some cultural depictions, developers can fundamentally misrepresent the context in which the aesthetic of a culture is developed. In this book and context, I use the term aesthetic/s to refer to the perceived look, style and way of something, someone or a group, such as taking on the aesthetics of a cultural group. For example, Mahuta (2012) discusses how the *Mark of Kri* (San Diego Studio, 2002), which is a Sony PlayStation 2 game, borrows heavily from Māori and other Pacific Islander cultures in the game's design and depictions. Mahuta (2012) discusses that throughout the game, there are aspects clearly taken from Māori culture. These Māori cultural elements include the build and depiction of the main character Rau and the marks in the game that need to be collected, which are heavily drawn from the Māori tā moko, a traditional Māori art of tattooing. The game also depicted the Māori taiaha, a uniquely Māori spear-like weapon. Mahuta (2012) points out how San Diego Studios clearly researched how they could create Māori characters, weapons and lore in the game. However, the problem is that such cultural objects and depictions do not include the context, language meaning and ways of knowing. In an interview with the art designer of the game, the designer indicated that *Mark of Kri* is not a depiction of Māori culture and the main character is not supposed to be Māori, stating "Rau's isn't Maori and he's not from or in New Zealand, so we kind of keep our ass covered that way. We apologize for any coincidences" (Perry, 2002). While the game does not claim to represent Māori culture, this approach removes the aesthetics of Māori culture from its original context and even denies that any of the obvious aesthetics and depictions were drawn from Māori culture.

Likewise, LaPensée (2008), in her examination of *Age of Empires III: Warchiefs* (Ensemble Studios, 2006), discusses how both in the aesthetic design of the game and the underlying gameplay mechanics, the game was clearly designed from a colonist perspective even while being placed in the role of First Nations in the Americas. In the past, the in-game mechanics were similar between European nations and Native American nations, such as mining metals, cutting down trees and so on. These actions are not necessarily representations of how different Indigenous nations might represent themselves or align with their philosophy (Age DE Team, 2020). In this game, the representation of Native American nations and communities is a representation of a colonist's understanding of Indigenous nations and communities. The fundamental issue is that even when depicted in-game, such games do not necessarily represent the deeper understandings or worldviews of the community they depict; instead, these games represent an essentialised view of how the developers think Indigenous people would view the world.

Torres Strait society – neighbouring interactions and trade relationships

The Torres Straits has various interactions and trade relationships with its neighbours, especially communities in Papua New Guinea (PNG). For example, there is a treaty in place between Torres Strait Islander communities and a number of coastal villages in PNG to facilitate trade and other traditional activities. People from these PNG communities would and, to this day, travel to the Torres Straits to trade with local communities. Torres Strait Islanders would trade with PNG people for their wood, which was of good quality, as well as other wooden items such as Warups and other artefacts. However, my father also recalls when PNG people had travelled as far as Waiben in large wooden boats. There are also interactions with Mainland Aboriginal communities as some Torres Strait stories feature Aboriginal people such as the Saga of Kuiam. Some Inner Island communities in the Torres Strait, such as the Kaurareg people, consider themselves Aboriginal people. Interactions with Asia have also very likely been in existence for some time. A Chinese ceramic dating as far back as 1500s–1600s has been found in the Torres Straits (Grave & McNiven, 2013). In TSVR, PNG traders are a central part of the storyline, as you must travel to the Top-Western Islands to obtain Warups, mats, Waps and spears from PNG traders.

Similarly, in *Europa Universalis IV* (*EUIV*; Paradox Development Studio, 2013), many nations were not represented and were instead depicted as blank pieces of land with minimal interactions and only for the purpose of being invaded and colonised. In this case, the representation is practically a non-representation or at least there is no representation in any meaningful way. That is, in a practical sense, a game representation of the colonial concept of Terra Nullius or nobody's land (Australian Institute of Aboriginal and Torres Strait Islander Studies, 2022). Nonetheless, while some Indigenous nations are depicted, the underlying game mechanics still strongly influence the player to play in a certain way to "win" the game. For example, if you were to play an Indigenous Australian nation or a Native American nation in *EUIV*, the game still encourages an empire-building approach, which actually reflects the historical actions that harmed and dispossessed the same Indigenous people. Only 8 years after the initial release and numerous patches did Paradox Interactive add playable nations to Australia, New Zealand and the Pacific Islands (Paradox Development Studio, 2013). However, even in these cases, players playing as Indigenous nations in the Pacific and the Americas are penalised heavily, making gameplay extremely hard and winning much harder than for European or most other nations in-game. In total, some representations of Indigenous nations are only presented through the lens of how the colonist would perceive them. In other cases, the historical significance of some Indigenous nations is denied outright by depicting their nations and lands as nothing else but places to be colonised.

Revisits and cultural redesigns by game designers

Encouragingly, there are examples where developers are returning to older games where the community criticised misrepresentations and developers then began working with communities to change cultural depictions in-game. For example, as discussed in the initial release of *Age of Empires III: Warchiefs* (Ensemble Studios, 2006), there was a nation called the Iroquois; however, after working with local people, the name was changed to the traditional name of the Haudenosaunee (Age DE Team, 2020; Talbot, 2020). A similar change happened to the Lakota people, also known previously as the Sioux. The developers also changed the mining mechanic in the game for Native American nations as mining was antithetical to Native American values and their respect for the earth and environment (Age DE Team, 2020). This in-game mechanic was replaced with another mechanic depicting the tribal market to generate coins (an in-game currency). A similar change happened to the Lakota nation to better represent the world view of these Indigenous communities.

Anthony Brave, an Indigenous consultant for the game, discusses how the Fire Pit (an in-game mechanic) harks back to old stereotypes where Native Americans are seen not as humans but as wild animals (Age DE Team, 2020; Talbot, 2020). The mechanics of the game are also starkly different depending on the played civilisation. For the Native American nations in-game, a fire pit would magically make native American units stronger while Western units gain strength through logical means such as developments in technology or developing capacity for war, such as through forts. In recent reworks, the fire pit was replaced with the Community Plaza for the Haudenosaunee, which consultants from the community felt was a truer depiction of their culture (Age DE Team, 2020). These changes are not just aesthetic changes, but changes that align with the common worldview of the cultures and communities in question, with members of those communities working with developers.

Criticisms of Pîhtokahanapiwiyin may have influenced 2K's development process as later downloadable content features the "Māori Empire" in *Civilization VI* (Firaxis Games, 2016), which is led by Kupe a Māori navigator who first arrived in Aotearoa (New Zealand). Apparently, the developers sought out experts to design the civilisation's facial tattoos, architecture, different buildings and monuments in-game. The developer also partnered with the head of a school at the Māori New Zealand Arts and Crafts Institute to design the tattoo of Kupe (Matt, 2018). Moreover, in a different take on the *Mortal Kombat* series, in the game *Killer Instinct*, the developers soon realised their depiction of Thunder, a Native American fighter, was inappropriate and based on the developers' limited understandings (Fahey, 2016). In response to this self-reflection, the developers worked with Indigenous consultants from the Pacific Northwest Nez Percé tribe whom the fictional character represented in-game. Various aspects were changed or removed, including headdresses that were more for ceremonial ev rather than combat to better reflect the culture and represent the cultural understandings of the actual community. These depictions, even after their redesign or change in approach, may not be perfect, but they do show a willingness and good will to involve communities in the game design processes and influence in-game representations of their own culture. There are other games, where the communities have been centrally involved from the very beginning of the game design process.

Cultural and community-centred game design

Video games such as *Never Alone* (Kisima Ingitchuna) (Upper One Games, 2014) have been praised for their deep and thoughtful representations of the Native Alaskan community. The game received public critical acclaim, winning various awards, including best debut game at the British Academy of Film and Television Arts in 2015 (British Academy of Film and Television Arts, 2015). This kind of praise and community support for *Never Alone* should be of no surprise as the game was developed by an Indigenous owned development company that worked with the community storytellers and Elders to develop the game (E-Line Media, 2016; Parkinson, 2014). Mulaka (Lienzo, 2018) was also developed through extensive involvement and consultation with Indigenous communities (Barasch, 2018). Other games include *When Rivers Were Trails* (The Indian Land Tenure Foundation, 2019) and *Thunderbird Strike* (LaPensée, 2017), whose developments were led and shaped by Elizabeth La-Pensée, an Anishinaabe game developer and scholar who worked closely with the community. See Figure 1.1 for a screenshot of *When Rivers Were Trails*.

Figure 1.1 Encountering an Oneida traveller in the player's own journey in *When Rivers Were Trails* (The Indian Land Tenure Foundation, 2019) [in-game screenshot].

In the public sphere, these games and their design approaches have been far better received by the communities that they depict in-game. Notably, these game development teams engaged and worked in consultation with the community from the very beginning of the design process. The significant change in these cases is the involvement of people from the culture or those with experience of the culture in the game development process. There may still be some problems of representation in the minds of the audience and how the players make sense of the cultural representation in-game. However, through community involvement, we can communicate a more direct and community-centred understanding of the culture to the players.

Flowers of the Torres Strait – the Hibiscus and Frangipani

Flowers are commonly depicted and used in Torres Strait art, carvings, clothing, wearables, tableware, decoration in the home, at events and on dance apparel. Two flowers in particular feature prominently on different objects and at different events. These flowers are the Hibiscus and Frangipani flowers. The hibiscus bark can also be used as weaving material (Wilson, 1988). The Frangipani tree features in stories such as the story of Pontianak who lives in a frangipani tree. See Figure 1.2 for a sketch of the flowers.

Figure 1.2 Hibiscus and frangipani flower that are important and commonly used in the Torres Straits and depicted in Torres Strait culture [sketch]. Sketch by Gehamat Loban. Year: 2022.

Culture and community as a response

The core of this representation issue seems to be from a limited understanding of the cultural context or a deep appreciation of the culture. In some games, the cultural depictions are aesthetic or shallow representations rather than the deeper worldview from the community. This argument is not to essentialise a community into one kind of representation, but clearly there are those from the community who call out games that do not match their understandings of their own culture, at least not in any deep or meaningful way. Community criticism frequently centres on a lack of community participation. Therefore, designer engagement with the community is an important part of not only representation of the community, but, as we will see further into the book, it is often an important part of cultural protocols for many communities.

If we do not consider how culture can be thoughtfully integrated into video games, there are consequences. Games that misrepresent cultures can essentialise cultures and perpetuate negative or harmful stereotypes. For game studios, they can face likely legitimate criticism that can affect the game's public image and create a frosty relationship between the developers and the community reflected in-game. This situation is not desirable, especially if the game is heavily centred around that culture. However, more critically, from a design perspective, designers miss out on accessing and integrating genuine and deep stories and reflections of culture into their games. In response to these challenges and opportunities, there are steps we can take to avoid creating negative and harmful stereotypes while engaging with and integrating the richer and deeper forms of the culture into games.

This book will articulate several steps to provide a framework and solution to these challenges and opportunities. To provide context to TSVR and my game design approach, Chapter 2 details a brief introduction and overview of the Torres Straits and its history centred around my own family's perspective and involvement. Community advocacy and strides for greater sovereignty form a part of this history, and community control of digital representations can be seen as a part of regaining sovereignty for some communities. While some misrepresentations in video games are non-depictions, others could be representations of the designer's limited knowledge and experiences with the culture. In either case, these depictions are typically surface-level reflections of the culture and often do not represent the culture in any deep or meaningful way. In Chapter 3, I use concepts from the Torres Straits to draw similar analogies, including the Torres Strait cultural palm representing deep culture and the Dogai symbolising a shallow representation of the culture. I use the palm and the Dogai to discuss the need to have a focus on deeper cultural reflections rather than surface-level depictions. Deep and surface cultures will be explained later in the book. In Chapter 4, I explore in-depth cultural design processes and considerations of TSVR. From there, I suggest that in order to access and better represent deeper culture in game depictions, there are three key practices worth considering: community participation, cultural immersion and rigorous research. Community participation is discussed in Chapter 5 and cultural immersion and rigorous research are covered in Chapter 6, along with the relationship of ethics to culture and games. See Figure 1.3 for a Venn diagram of the different combinations of approaches to integrating culture into game design. Chapter 7 concludes with key messages and suggestions from the book.

THREE MEASURED APPROACH VENN DIAGRAM

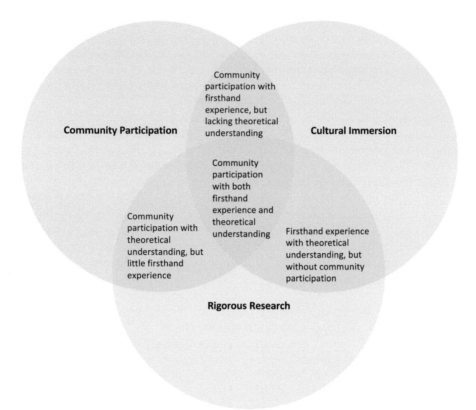

Figure 1.3 This Venn diagram shows three approaches to embedding culture into game design, including community participation, cultural immersion and rigorous research. Cultural immersion without community participation or rigorous research only provides an outside perspective of the culture. Rigorous research without community involvement or the designer's own cultural immersion is just a theoretical understanding of the culture. Community participation even by itself is a strong approach, but can be further enhanced by the designer's own understanding through cultural immersion and theoretical frameworks to support real experiences. Ideally, a game development project that includes all three approaches supporting each other would be the best outcome [graphical diagram].

Conclusion

This chapter has introduced the definition of culture and briefly explored issues around cultural representations in historical literary, artistic and academic works, and how this issue has continued into video games. Culture can form a significant part of a person's identity and can be seen as a way of life for many people. However, different cultures and communities have often been historically represented in various literature, art and research by those from outside the community, often in exaggerated and biased ways. These tendencies of misrepresenting cultures and communities, even unwittingly, have continued into the design and production of video games. However, there have been shifts in game design approaches around cultural representations, with some game studios returning to redesign poor cultural depictions in conjunction with the communities they depicted. In other cases, some game developers are involving the community from the ground up in the game design, with positive results and receptions from the communities themselves and wider audiences. Therefore, a thoughtful approach is required in the design of games with cultural representations.

The issue of cultural representation could be seen as an epistemological issue. Epistemology is the theory of knowledge; however, more relevant to this discussion, we can pose the question of how knowledge is constructed or produced. We are all constructing knowledge differently from each other in our own minds. However, designers are then representing that constructed knowledge in video games. Adding to this process, players then make their own sense of the represented knowledge through interaction with the game. Therefore, the issue is how can we better represent the knowledge of the culture in video games and also better construct knowledge of the culture in the players' minds as well as in our own minds as designers. We cannot directly control how the players make sense of the game and how they construct knowledge of the culture through the game. The players' constructions of the knowledge will always be in relation to their own experiences. Yet by constructing richer and more crystallised knowledge of the cultures in our own minds, our enhanced knowledge may flow into better in-game cultural representations. Then, through our enriched knowledge and other adjustments to design practices, we may be able to embed deeper knowledge of the culture in-game and create interactive environments that encourage fuller cultural representations in the minds of the audience. Therefore, from our end as designers, we need to put measures in place to ensure a fuller and more thoughtful construction of knowledge in our own minds and in how we represent such knowledge in-game.

My main proposition is that those involved in developing games be thoughtful about how culture is embedded in video games and the design process. This proposition need not preclude game designers from being involved in creating depictions of cultures to which they do not belong. However, it requires more thoughtfulness and consideration of how cultures may be represented in-game. A sound approach to culture is the inclusion of those who have the cultural experience, namely, the communities themselves. This approach means that the deeper experiences and worldview of culture accumulated through their lives can be represented in a true sense rather than just through quick research on the internet. The practice of cultural immersion is for the designer to better understand the culture, and a better conceptualisation of the culture will flow into deeper reflections of culture and community in-game. Rigorous research also supports the construction of knowledge about a culture and asks designers to think critically about the kinds of materials they are using to build their game worlds. In addition, we are often not aware or reflexive of how we are representing other cultures. Therefore, being aware of the difficulties of cultural representations within video games (and broader digital media) and recognising that it is an issue are already part of the journey in mitigating the issue. Before I discuss the theoretical framework of culture and representations, I would like to provide context for TSVR and briefly cover a foundational introduction to the Torres Straits with a focus on geography and history to convey the distinctiveness and vibrancy of the culture and way of life.

References

ABC News. (2016). *Survival Island 3: Game that purportedly calls for players to kill Aboriginal people prompts outrage.* https://www.abc.net.au/news/2016-01-16/racist-survival-island-3-game-taken-down-from-appstores/7092782

Age DE Team. (2020). *An interview with Age of Empires III: DE Consultant, Anthony Brave.* https://www.ageofempires.com/news/interview-anthony-brave/

Australian Institute of Aboriginal and Torres Strait Islander Studies. (2022). *The Mabo case.* https://aiatsis.gov.au/explore/mabo-case

Baker, K. (2013). *Information literacy and cultural heritage: Developing a model for lifelong learning.* Elsevier.

Barasch, A. (2018). *'Mulaka': Struggle of exploring Tarahumara Lore in a video game.* https://variety.com/2018/gaming/features/mulaka-mexico-lienzo-developer-1202749723/

Beckett, J. (1990). *Torres Strait Islanders: Custom and colonialism.* Cambridge University Press.

Brayboy, B. M., Gough, H. R., Leonard, B., Roehl, R., & Solyom, J. A. (2012). Reclaiming scholarship: Critical indigenous research methodologies. In. S. D. Lapan, M. L. T. Quartoli, & F. J. Riemer (Eds.), *Qualitative research: An introduction to methods and designs* (pp. 423–450). Jossey-Bass.

British Academy of Film and Television Arts. (2015). *Games | debut game in 2015.* https://awards.bafta.org/award/2015/games/debut-game

Brumann, C. (2015). Cultural heritage. In J. D. Wright (Ed.), *International encyclopedia of the social & behavioral sciences* (2nd ed., pp. 414–419). Elsevier. https://doi.org/10.1016/B978-0-08-097086-8.12185-3

Campbell, C. (2018). Cree Nation headman unhappy with Civilization 6 portrayal. *Polygon.* https://www.polygon.com/2018/1/4/16850906/cree-nation-civilization-6-poundmaker

Connaughton, M. (2016). Meet the developer behind Australia's most hated game. *Vice.* https://www.vice.com/en/article/kw93yy/we-spoke-to-the-man-who-made-australias-most-hated-game

Connell, R. (2018). Decolonizing sociology. *Contemporary Sociology, 47*(4), 399–407. https://doi.org/10.1177/0094306118779811

E-Line Media. (2016). *Never Alone official website.* http://neveralonegame.com/

Elu, M. (2004). Cooking, walking, and talking cosmology: An Islander woman's perspective of religion. In R. Davis (Ed.), *Woven histories, dancing lives: Torres Strait Islander identity, culture and history* (p. 140). Aboriginal Studies Press. https://search.informit.org/doi/10.3316/informit.008918914255709

Ensemble Studios (2006). *Age of empires III: The WarChiefs* [video game]. Microsoft Game Studios.

Fahey, M. (2016). *Killer Instinct's Thunder gets a more culturally accurate outfit.* https://www.kotaku.com.au/2016/12/killer-instincts-thunder-gets-a-more-culturally-accurate-outfit/

Firaxis Games. (2016). *Civilization VI* [video game]. 2K games.

Gallagher, P., Mckinlay, E., Pullon, S., & McHugh, P. (2019). Student perceptions of cultural immersion during an interprofessional programme. *Journal of Interprofessional Care*, *33*(2), 264–266.

Gérôme, J.-L. (1866). *The slave market* [painting]. Clark Art Institute. https://www.clarkart.edu/artpiece/detail/slave-market

Gérôme, J.-L. (1879). *The snake charmer* [painting]. Clark Art Institute. https://www.clarkart.edu/artpiece/detail/snake-charmer

Grave, P., & McNiven, I. J. (2013). Geochemical provenience of 16th–19th century CE Asian ceramics from Torres Strait, northeast Australia. *Journal of Archaeological Science*, *40*(12), 4538–4551.

Hutchinson, R. (2019). *Japanese Culture through videogames*. Routledge.

LaPensée, B. A. (2008). Signifying the west: Colonialist design in Age of Empires III: The WarChiefs. *Eludamos. Journal for Computer Game Culture*, *2*(1), 129–144.

LaPensée, E. (2017). *Thunderbird strike* [video game].

LaPensée, E. A., Laiti, O., & Longboat, M. (2022). Towards sovereign games. *Games and Culture*, *17*(3), 328–343.

Lienzo. (2018). *Mulaka* [video game].

Longboat, M. (2019). *Terra Nova: Enacting videogame development through indigenous-led creation*. Concordia University.

Lowe, L. (2018). 3. Orient as woman, orientalism as sentimentalism: Flaubert. In *Critical terrains* (pp. 75–101). Cornell University Press.

Mahuta, D. (2012). Māori in video games-a digital identity. *Te Kaharoa*, *5*(1).

Maroney, K. (2001). My entire waking life. *The Games Journal*. http://www.thegamesjournal.com/articles/MyEntireWakingLife.shtml. Access date 16 Jan 2023.

Matt, S. (2018). *On bringing the Māori to civilization VI*. https://www.digitallydownloaded.net/2018/12/on-bringing-the-maori-to-civilization-vi.html

Midway (1995). *Mortal Kombat 3* [video game]. Midway.

Myers, L. J. (1987). The deep structure of culture: Relevance of traditional African culture in contemporary life. *Journal of Black Studies*, *18*(1), 72–85.

N A. (2016). *Killing Indigenous Australians is not a game!* https://www.change.org/p/amazon-killing-indigenous-australians-is-not-a-game

NIL Entertainment. (2015). *Survival island 3: Australia story* [video game].

Paradox Development Studio (2013). *Europa Universalis IV* [video game]. Paradox Interactive.

Parkinson, H. J. (2014). *Alaska's indigenous game Never Alone teaches co-operation through stories*. The Guardian.

Pelegrini, S. (2008). World heritage sites, types and laws. In D. M. Pearsall (Ed.), *Encyclopedia of archaeology* (pp. 2215–2218). Academic Press. https://doi.org/10.1016/B978-012373962-9.00323-X

Penix-Tadsen, P. (2016). *Cultural code: Video games and Latin America*. MIT press.

Perry, D. C. (2002). *Interview with Jeff Merghart*. IGN. https://www.ign.com/articles/2002/07/18/interview-with-jeff-merghart

Printup, C. A. (2019). *Oregon Trail to Assassin's Creed: Right and wrong Native American portrayals in video games*. https://indiancountrytoday.com/lifestyle/oregon-trail-to-assassins-creed-right-and-wrong-native-american-portrayals-in-video-games

Said, E. (1978). *Orientalism*. Routledge.

San Diego Studio. (2002). *The mark of Kri* [video game]. Sony Computer Entertainment.

Singe, J. (1979). *The Torres Strait: People and history*. University of Queensland Press.

Smith, E. A., & Bird, R. L. B. (2000). Turtle hunting and tombstone opening: Public generosity as costly signaling. *Evolution and Human Behavior*, *21*(4), 245–261.

Talbot, C. (2020). *Age of Empires 3: DE changes Native American, First Nations civs' mining to a marketplace.* https://www.pcgamesn.com/age-of-empires-iii-definitive-edition/mining-changes

The Indian Land Tenure Foundation. (2019). *When rivers were trails* [video game].

Upper One Games (2014). *Never alone* [video game]. E-Line Media.

Williams, R. (1983). *Keywords: A vocabulary of culture and society.* In: Fontana Press.

Willis, K. G. (2014). Chapter 7 – The use of stated preference methods to value cultural heritage. In V. A. Ginsburgh & D. Throsby (Eds.), *Handbook of the economics of art and culture* (Vol. 2, pp. 145–181). Elsevier. https://doi.org/10.1016/B978-0-444-53776-8.00007-6

Wilson, L. (1988). *Thathilgaw Emeret Lu: A handbook of traditional Torres Strait Islands material culture.* Department of Education.

2 Knowing the context

A Torres Strait perspective

In Australia, there are two groups of Indigenous people, Aboriginal people and Torres Strait Islander people. The Torres Straits is a large collection of islands and waters located between two landmasses, Australia and Papua New Guinea. The Torres Straits is positioned where the Pacific and Indian Oceans meet and there are 133 Islands, sandy cays and rocky outcrops of which 38 are homes for Torres Strait communities (Torres Shire Council, 2022a). The Torres Straits has a long and vibrant history with many people and cultures influencing Torres Strait identity and the islands, in part due to its location, ecosystem and geography. Influences on Torres Strait culture can be seen as originating from islander inter-actions and trade with Papuan and Mainland Aboriginal people, engagement and conflict with European and Pacific Islander missionaries and cultural exchanges with indentured labourers from Asia who worked in the pearling industry. Each of these interactions with other communities has left their cultural imprint on the Torres Strait community and has helped shape contemporary Torres Strait identity. However, even with these diverse interactions, Torres Strait Islanders maintain a strong connection with their local place and the surrounding land, sky and sea as Indigenous people.

I believe that in order to understand my design approach to TSVR, it is impor-tant to understand the contextual and foundational information of the community and place being represented in-game. In this chapter, I have provided a small and introductory understanding of the people and the geography of the Torres Straits, so that you as the reader can better understand discussions about the way of life and the stories of the Torres Straits. As designers, the understandings in this chap-ter may be similar to foundational knowledge that you will need for your own approach to integrating culture into a game development project. That is who the people are, where they are and what are the stories that make up their history. I hope that the chapter draws your attention to the need to involve community and acknowledge how community see themselves, before you as the designer represent those very same people in your games.

This chapter is dedicated to a short overview of the Torres Strait contempo-rary community and history of the Torres Straits. The first section discusses the general geography, communities and languages of the Torres Straits to provide a

DOI: 10.1201/9781003276289-3

broad understanding of the Torres Straits in relation to the Pacific and the rest of the world. The second section provides a brief historical overview of the Torres Straits community, largely from the perspective of my family. Rather than trying to cover the entire history of the Torres Straits, I felt the most direct and personal way to cover Torres Strait Islander history is from my own family's perspective of events and their involvement with community. The islands have a long history, but prominent aspects of Torres Strait Islander history from my family's perspective include the pearling industry (Beckett, 1990; Kerr, 2010; Ohshima, 1988; Singe, 1979), national service (Gaffney, 1989), working on the railroads (Western Australian Museum, 2022) and the development and gaining autonomy for the Torres Straits (Gaffney, 1989, 2015). Finally, I will discuss how these historical actions and events form a significant part of the cultural memory of the Torres Straits and the movement for greater recognition and autonomy of the region. Cultural memory can involve recalling and reflecting on experiences, constructing memories and then ascribing meaning to those memories to then pass on as cultural understandings to the next generations (Apaydin, 2020; Van Dijck, 2004). Part of this cultural memory is the service to the community and how this forms a part of exercising autonomy for the community to control our own fate. I see Torres Strait Virtual Reality, the game I led the development of, as a very small part of this exercise in digital media where we can better shape our own representation and new cultural production within a digital space.

Torres Strait geography, languages and lifestyle

The name of the Torres Straits comes from the Spanish navigator Luis Vaez de Torres who travelled through our waters in 1606 (Australian Institute of Aboriginal and Torres Strait Islander Studies, 2022a). Many Islanders also use the term Zenadth Kes which was created by Ephraim Bani, a very senior and highly respected Torres Strait knowledge holder and linguist. Both Zenadth Kes and Torres Strait are used to refer to the region and people, especially the latter when engaging with outsiders in everyday conversation. As a Torres Strait Islander, I more often identity myself and other Torres Strait Islanders through our family and the Island of our lineage. Although many Torres Strait Islanders live outside of the Torres Straits for reasons such as work and education, our identity typically remains very strongly connected to our culture and our home islands and waters.

The Torres Straits is located between Cape York in the farthest point of Queensland Australia and Papua New Guinea as shown in Figure 2.1. There are many islands that vary in their size, geography and habitat. The Torres Straits region tends to be divided into five island groups with each group speaking different dialects (Gur a Baradharaw Kod, 2022; Torres Strait Regional Authority, 2022). See Figure 2.2 for a map depiction of the Torres Straits and a general division of the five island groups plus the Torres Strait communities in the North Peninsula Area (NPA) on the Australian mainland. The division of the five island groups tend to be around the Torres Strait cultural practices, location, geography and language. There are two traditional language groups in the Torres Straits, the Kala Lagaw Ya

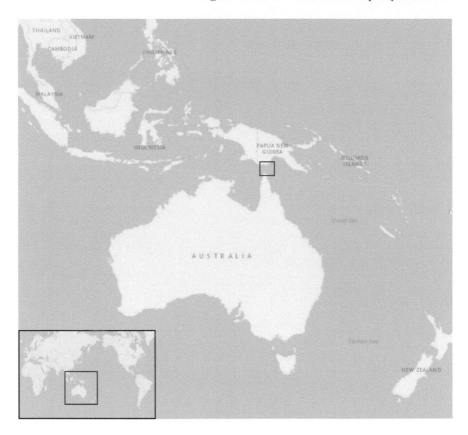

Figure 2.1 Map of Australia and Pacific neighbours with the Torres Straits highlighted in red and a mini map of the world in the bottom left corner (Queensland Government, 2023) [Map]. Modified from *Queensland Globe*, © State of Queensland 2023, licensed under CC BY 4.0. from the State of Queensland.

(KLY) and Miriam Mir/Mer. The Eastern group traditionally speaks Miriam Mir/Mer while the Top Western, Western, Central and Inner Island groups speak the KLY language.

The Top Western group is in the north-west of the Torres Straits and speak a dialect of KLY called Kalaw Kawaw Ya (Gur a Baradharaw Kod, 2022; Torres Strait Regional Authority, 2022). Within the Top Western, there are three islands with established communities which are Saibai, Boigu and Dauan. Saibai is a flat mud island that has a large interior of swamps with brackish waters (Torres Strait Island Regional Council, 2018b). The formation of the island can be traced back to the Fly River in Papua New Guinea that releases large quantities of silt and sediment into the nearby waters and coastal area. Sabai has been subjected to king tides which have caused many Saibai communities to relocate to Cape York to avoid the danger, but enable them to still be close to their home (Torres Strait Island Regional Council, 2016m). Boigu similarly is a low-lying island, prone to flooding and has

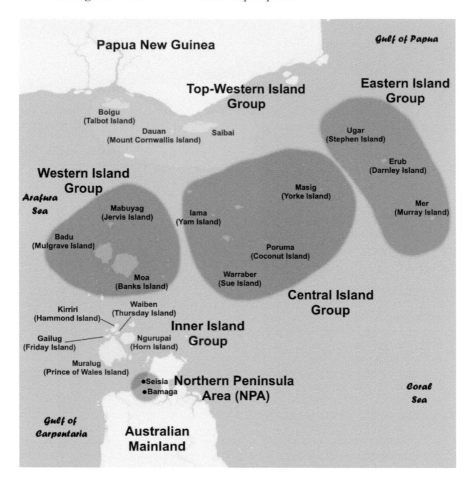

Figure 2.2 Map of the Torres Straits with the five island groups highlighted plus mainland
Torres Strait communities (Queensland Government, 2023) [Map]. Modified
from *Queensland Globe,* © State of Queensland 2023, licensed under CC BY
4.0. from the State of Queensland.

been subject to tidal waves (Torres Strait Island Regional Council, 2016c).
Also given the geography of Boigu, the island has sparse plant life and is mainly
swamp land with the growth of coastal mangroves that help protect the island from
sea erosion. In contrast to Saibai and Boigu, Dauan is a rocky granite island and is
the most northerly granite peak of Australia as well as maintaining the highest
granite peak in the Torres Straits of up to 300 metres high (Torres Strait Island
Regional Council, 2016d). The soil is relatively fertile, and the island maintains
permanent cool freshwater springs which all help support local gardens. Given the
proximity to mainland Papua New Guinea, many Islanders from the Top-Western
Island group have family, kinship and cultural ties to Papuan people and communities. The proximity to the mainland of Papua New Guinea also affects the materials

used in the production of different objects. For example, cassowary feathers might often be used to create a Dhoeri.

Torres Strait headdress – the Dhoeri or Dhari

The Dhoeri or Dhari is a headdress worn for dances, ceremonies, performances and celebrations. Communities from the KLY language groups tend to call the headdress a Dhoeri while those from the Meriam Mer language group tend to call it a Dhari. Dhoeris may vary in size, shape and materials used from island to island. For example, Dhoeris from the Top-Western Island Group may be constructed with Cassowary feathers given its proximity to Papua New Guinea which have Cassowaries. However, the Dhoeri is universal across the Torres Straits and represents strong links to the region as well as a sense of belonging. The Dhoeri symbol is also depicted on the official Torres Strait flag. See Figure 2.3 for a photograph of two different Dhoeris.

Figure 2.3 Myself holding two different kinds of Dhoeris. The one on the left is typical of the Eastern Island group, while the one on the right is more typical of Western Island group [photograph].

The Western Island group is located in the west of the Torres Straits and they speak the KLY Mabuyag dialect (Gur a Baradharaw Kod, 2022; Torres Strait Regional Authority, 2022). In the Western Island group there are also three islands with established communities, Badu (Mulgrave Island), Mabuyag (Jervis Island) and Moa (Kubin and St Pauls communities). Badu has rocky ridges and sandy parts as well as light vegetation (Torres Strait Island Regional Council, 2016b, 2018a; Wilson, 1993). Pearlers were also established on the island during the pearling industry. Like Badu, Mabuyag is a continental island and has basaltic rock mounds on parts of the island with some vegetation (Torres Strait Island Regional Council, 2016h). Similarly, Moa has mounds of rock and is lightly covered with plant life, but has two separate communities on the island (Torres Strait Island Regional Council, 2016a, 2016p). The St Pauls (Wug) community at the Northern end of the island, and the Kubin (Arkai) community that is located on the south side of the island. Moa is the second-largest island in the Torres Straits. These three islands are a part of an old submerged land bridge from Cape York to Papua New Guinea.

The Central Island group is located in the centre of the Torres Straits and they speak the Kulkalgau Ya dialect of KLY (Gur a Baradharaw Kod, 2022; Torres Strait Regional Authority, 2022). The Central Island group has four established island communities, Masig (Yorke Island), Poruma (Coconut Island), Warraber (Sue Island) and Iama (Yam Island). Masig Island is a coral cay island and historically was a central point for trade networks in the Torres Straits (Torres Strait Island Regional Council, 2016i). Poruma is also a coral cay island, but is a narrow and long Island with shallow coral reefs around the island's fringes (Queensland Government, 2018b; Torres Strait Island Regional Council, 2016l). Warraber Island is a coral cay island and features an abundance of traditional fruits such as Wongai (Torres Strait) plums and coconuts (Torres Strait Island Regional Council, 2016o). Iama Island, unlike the other central islands, is not a coral cay island but rather a continental island formed on granite basement rocks (Torres Strait Island Regional Council, 2016f; Torres Strait Regional Authority, 2013).

The Inner Island group is located in the south and close to Cape York which is the tip of the mainland of Australia (Gur a Baradharaw Kod, 2022; Torres Strait Regional Authority, 2022). The Inner Island group speak the Kaurareg dialect which is a part of the KLY language group. The Inner Islands have five island communities Muralug (Prince of Wales Island), Ngurupai (Horn Island), Gailug (Friday Island), Kirriri (Hammond Island) and Waiben (Thursday Island). Muralug is a hilly island with pleasant beaches and is the largest island in the Torres Straits with a variety of wildlife including deer. Ngurupai is a hilly island with rocks and greenery. Ngurupai maintains the main airstrip for outside visitors when visiting the Torres Straits. Gailug has many scenic beaches, sand hills and is where a pearl culture farm is located and attracts tourists. Kirriri is a hilly island that is a short ferry ride from Waiben (Torres Strait Island Regional Council, 2016g). Waiben is a hilly island with scenic beaches and deep surrounding waters which serve as an excellent port for large ships. Because of these deep-seated waters off the island, Waiben Island is the main administrative and commercial hub of the Torres Straits (Torres Shire Council, 2022b). See Figures 2.4 and 2.5 for photographs of Waiben. Close to the Inner Island group is the Northern Peninsula Area on Cape York mainland

Figure 2.4 Waiben from a hill view [photograph]. Year: Circa 1950s–1960s.

Figure 2.5 Waiben from Muralug at sunset [photograph]. Year: Circa 1970s.

Australia, there are two predominantly Torres Strait communities, Bamaga and Seisia (Torres Strait Regional Authority, 2022). In these two communities, you find many people from the Top-Western Island group who have sought refuge from the King Tides that affect the islands. However, many other people from the other islands have joined the community. The Island communities are very grateful to the local Aboriginal communities who allowed them to live on their land.

The Eastern Island group is located in the east of the Torres Straits and this island group is the place where Miriam Mir/Mer language is traditionally spoken. Within the Miriam Mir/Mer language, there are two dialects, the Erub/Ugar dialect and the Mer dialect (Gur a Baradharaw Kod, 2022; Torres Strait Regional Authority, 2022). The Eastern Island group has three established island communities, Mer (Murray Island), Ugar (Stephen Island), Erub (Darnley Island). Mer is an island formed from an extinct volcano with rich soil which is suitable for gardens (Torres Strait Island Regional Council, 2016j). Mer is also home to Eddie Mabo who started the Native Title land rights claim and won, allowing other Torres Strait and Aboriginal communities to follow suit (Australian Institute of Aboriginal and Torres Strait Islander Studies, 2022b). Erub is an island of volcanic origin, but the area also has pearl clams and beche-de-mer which have attracted pearlers and beche-de-mer gatherers to visit the island (Torres Strait Island Regional Council, 2016e). These industries attracted people from the Pacific, Philippines and Malay Archipelago who married local women and imprinted their culture on Torres Strait culture. Ugar is also an island of volcanic origin with rich soil and dense plant life and one of the region's smallest communities (Torres Strait Island Regional Council, 2016n). A summary of the islands and their features can be seen in Table 2.1.

Table 2.1 Torres Strait Island groups, names, languages and geography (Duce et al., 2010; Gur a Baradharaw Kod, 2022; Torres Strait Regional Authority, 2022; Wilson, 1993)

Island Group	Island Name	European Name	Traditional Language and Dialect	Island Geography Type
Top-Western Island Group	Boigu	Talbot Island	KLY – Kalaw Kawaw Ya Dialect	Low Lying Mangrove Swamp Island
	Dauan	Mount Cornwallis Island	KLY – Kalaw Kawaw Ya Dialect	Continental Island
	Saibai	N/A	KLY – Kalaw Kawaw Ya Dialect	Low Lying Mangrove Swamp Island
Western Island Group	Badu	Mulgrave Island	KLY – Mabuyag Dialect	Continental Island
	Mabuyag	Jervis Island	KLY – Mabuyag Dialect	Continental Island
	Moa (St Paul and Kubin communities)	Banks Island	KLY – Mabuyag Dialect	Continental Island

(*Continued*)

Table 2.1 (Continued)

Island Group	Island Name	European Name	Traditional Language and Dialect	Island Geography Type
Central Island Group	Masig	Yorke Island	KLY – Kulkalgau Ya Dialect	Coral Cay Reef Island
	Poruma	Coconut Island	KLY – Kulkalgau Ya Dialect	Coral Cay Reef Island
	Warraber	Sue Island	KLY – Kulkalgau Ya Dialect	Coral Cay Reef Island
	Iama	Yam Island	KLY – Kulkalgau Ya Dialect	Continental Island
Eastern Island Group	Mer	Murray Island	Meriam Mir/ Mer – Mer Dialect	Island of Volcanic Origin
	Ugar	Stephen Island	Meriam Mir/ Mer – Erub/ Ugar Dialect	Island of Volcanic Origin
	Erub	Darnley Island	Meriam Mir/ Mer – Erub/ Ugar Dialect	Island of Volcanic Origin
Inner Island Group	Kirriri	Hammond Island	KLY – Kaurareg Dialect	Continental Island
	Muralug	Prince of Wales	KLY – Kaurareg Dialect	Continental Island
	Ngurupai	Horn Island	KLY – Kaurareg Dialect	Continental Island
	Waiben	Thursday Island	KLY – Kaurareg Dialect	Continental Island
	Gailug	Friday Island	KLY – Kaurareg Dialect	Continental Island
Northern Peninsula Area (NPA) Communities	Seisia	N/A	KLY – Kalaw Kawaw Ya Dialect, but also other languages and dialects	Australian Mainland
	Bamaga	N/A	KLY – Kalaw Kawaw Ya Dialect, but also other languages and dialects	Australian Mainland

KLY and Meriam Mer are the two original languages of the Torres Straits and are still spoken on the outer and regional islands. However, in the Inner Island group, Torres Strait creole is now widely spoken and is gaining more popularity in the region. Torres Strait creole is an English-based language but also uses words from the original island languages, Papua New Guinea languages, Aboriginal languages, Malay languages and more. Torres Strait creole resulted from European invasion and colonisation of the region, but the language was also shaped by interaction and trade with various Papua New Guinea and Aboriginal communities. Creole has also been influenced by indentured labourers brought and attracted to the region from Indonesia, Malaysia, the Philippines, Japan and many other places. There are also likely words from other Pacific Islands as many other Islanders were intermediaries for the London Missionary Society when they established themselves on the islands to convert the Torres Strait communities to Christianity. Thus, there are two traditional languages with various dialects spoken in the Torre Straits, particularly on the outer islands with Torres Strait creole commonly spoken throughout the Torres Straits.

Torres Strait culture is intimately connected to the land and sky, but especially the sea. Much of the food for many communities is obtained from the sea and many of our totems are sea animals. The islands and the surrounding sea and reefs are home to a plethora of diverse and vibrant ecosystems and marine animals, including dugong and various turtles (Green, Hawksbill and Flatback Sea), and was the central location of the world's pearling Industry (Torres Strait Island Regional Council, 2016k). Fishing is part of a way of life in the Torres Straits, and one can catch various types of fish from sandy shore fish to reef fish to pelagic fish in the open ocean. Hunting for turtles and dugong are also a part of the culture and are particularly important for festivals such as weddings, funerals and Tombstone Openings. We have sustainably hunted and fished for generations and respect ocean life as totemic creatures. In the islands, we often dive to collect bech-de-mer (sea cucumber) or spearfish for various marine animals such as crayfish. My father would tell me how he when the tide went down, he could search for crabs and octopus for a meal. He even told me how the receding tide also uncovered shipwrecks which he would search for and strip metal from the wrecks to sell to the copper monger. For myself, I was not completely raised in the Torres Straits, but my way of life and childhood growing up was strongly connected to Torres Strait culture and the water.

Torres Strait knowledge – seasonal calendar

Torres Straits Islanders have a strong association with the land, the sea and the sky of the Torres Straits and these intimate connections help formulate the understanding of the region's seasons (Gab Titui Cultural Centre, 2022). In the Torres Straits, there are generally four seasons, Kuki, Waur/Sager, Naigai and Zey. The Kuki Season is associated with North-West winds which are strong winds and blow from January until April each year. The Kuki season is also the wet monsoon season. Waur/Sager is associated with the South-East trade winds and blows from May until December. Waur/Sager is typically known as a dry season. Naigai (Nay gay) is associated with the Northerly wind and typically blows from October until December each year. Naigai is known for when its heat and humidity are at the highest. Zey are southern winds that blow randomly throughout the year.

In total, the Torres Straits is a highly diverse region geographically, linguistically and culturally. Each of the five island groups are geographically unique and linguistically different with varied languages and dialects. The local Torres Strait communities are intimately connected to and have deep knowledge of the surrounding land, sky and sea. These intimate connections to the surroundings manifest in a life often centred around the ocean with many islanders having marine life as their totems. However, Torres Strait Islanders are bound together through a shared Torres Strait identity and history.

Torres Strait history from a family perspective

The Torres Straits has a long history, however, I wish to focus part of my discussion of Torres Strait history predominantly around my own family's history in relation to the Torres Strait as that is what I know most fully. Much of the information I discuss in regards to family history came directly from my family and through a few documented sources of my Nene (grandmother) Ellie Gaffney's books called *Somebody Now* (Gaffney, 1989) and *Mura Solwata Kosker: We Saltwater Women* (Gaffney, 2015). Nene Ellie Gaffney will be discussed later in the chapter. Another source used is *Eseli's Notebook* (Eseli et al., 1998). From oral history as well as these books, I can trace my earliest lineage to my forefather Peid.

Torres Strait scholarship – Eseli's Notebook

Eseli's Notebook is an account of Torres Strait natural science, clan territory, kinship links and family lineages (Eseli et al., 1998). Eseli's Notebook was primarily written by Peter Eseli who was a Torres Strait Islander from Mabuyag. Peter Eseli was born in February 1886 and died on 16 September 1958 at Bamaga, in Cape York where he is now buried. Although written earlier, the notebook was likely completed around 1939 or later. The notebook is thought to be the first scholarly manuscript from an Indigenous Australian person (Eseli et al., 1998). Given this fact, the notebook is of cultural importance to Torres Strait Islanders, wider Indigenous Australia, and the broader Australian society. Eseli wrote the book in KLY (Kala Lagaw Ya) and the book was later translated and transcribed into English for wider access.

Peid is the earliest family member I can trace back eight generations (likely alive in the late 1700s or early 1800s) who is on my fathers' family from Mabuyag (Eseli et al., 1998; Gaffney, 1989). This lineage is my Dato (grandfather's) line whose totem is the dangal (dugong) from Mabuyag. My other totem is daibau (yam) which is from the Boigu family line. Peid was the headman of Panai which is a community on the Island of Mabuyag. Peid had a son called Ngari. Ngari then had a son called Peidia (Petha) who married a woman named Umi and they had a girl named Dadu. Dadu is my great great Nene (grandmother). It was during Dadu's lifetime that the London Missionary Society (LMS) inserted and established itself on the island (around 1872) in an effort to Christianise the people of Mabuyag (Queensland Government, 2018a).

When the LMS colonised the islands, it was not just European people, but also Christian converts from the Pacific Islands such as those in New Caledonia who were used as intermediaries between the Torres Strait people and European people. These Pacific Islander people add another layer of culture to the Torres Straits and different parts of Torres Strait culture have been influenced by the Pacific Islander culture such as the words in songs (e.g. Sesere eeye) as well as the aesthetics and structures of the architecture and housing in the Torres Straits (David & Ash, 2008). These Pacific Islander people have had their influence on the Torres Strait that can be seen in contemporary Torres Strait Islander culture today.

Nonetheless, it was during this time that Dadu had a daughter name Gerti (Gertrude) who was born at sea near Christmas Island 1893. In adulthood, Great Nene Gerti married Great Dato Tom Loban (Simeon Sardir) who was an Indonesian man from Banda Neira. They had four children who lived into adulthood, Talep (Ted), Jean Non, Frank and Ellie. My Great Dato Tom Loban had several jobs throughout his lifetime, but he was particularly involved in the pearling industry in the Torres Straits, especially as a pearl shell grader. The pearling industry had a huge impact on the lives of Torres Strait Islanders with many islanders working in the industry and the industry bringing many people from Asia to the islands.

Torres Strait art – popular traditional songs

Torres Strait songs are often used to tell stories, capture history or communicate valuable lessons. Most Torres Strait songs have accompanying dances and hand movements which are interlinked with the story, history or lesson being communicated through the song. There are many traditional songs from the Torres Strait that have been popularised and are sung and practiced by many people from around the world. A few popularised songs are listed here:

- Taba Naba is a song and sit-down dance about going down to the water and to the reef in a dinghy and having fun.
- Sesere Eeye is a well know Torres Strait song and dance that is good for teaching children and adults alike. The song is about a kingfisher bird and the clapping hand movements in the dance act out the bird's beak snapping. Some of the words used in the song are from other Pacific Islands.
- Inanay Kapuana is another Torres Strait Islander song, but the song is also shared and sung by some Aboriginal communities on the mainland.

Pearling industry

During and even prior to the LMS process to Christianise the islands, there were European seafarers and boats searching for beche-de-mer and pearl shells around Mabuyag and in the wider Torres Straits (Queensland Government, 2018a). During the late 1800s to mid-1900s, the Torres Straits became a central hub for the Australian and even global pearling industry (State Library of Queensland, 2014). Pearl shells were used in various ways including for clothing buttons, combs, jewellery, insets in furniture, and cutlery handle decorations and various other products (State Library of Queensland, 2014). The pearling industry in the Torres Straits and other pearling sites in Northern Australia, such as Broome, supplied the majority of the world's demand for pearl shell at the time. See Figure 2.6 for a photograph of a diver collecting pearl shell. However, the industry died with the introduction of plastics which replaced the use of pearl shells in clothing buttons and other products.

The boom of the pearling trade brought workers from all over the world, but in particular from Asia to work in the pearling industry. People from Indonesia,

Figure 2.6 Diver in a suit collecting and placing pearl shells in basket to be lifted up to the pearling lugger in the Torres Straits (Hurley, 1921) [photograph]. Photography by Frank Hurley. Year: Circa between 1921 and 1939.

Malaysia, the Philippines, Japan, Sri Lanka and many other places came to the Torres Straits. At that time, this large migration created a highly multicultural society where "'there were Japanese divers, barefoot Malays in loose sarongs, Chinese in blue trousers, skull caps and pigtails', selling 'turtle steaks, which they carried draped over bamboo poles', Japanese women in kimonos, a Japanese temple near the Post Office, a tiny tin Buddhist temple and an equally small Chinese Joss house" (Shnukal & Ramsay, 2017, p. 41). The people of these different cultures contributed and intermarried with many of the local island people to create the highly syncretic Torres Strait culture that we have today. The influence of these people from Asia can be seen in many aspects of life from the dishes to clothing to the games played on the islands (e.g. the game Dadu). However, while many workers came voluntarily, others were not and instead were often kidnapped from their homes even as children and forced into slavery in the form of indentured labour within the pearling industry.

Torres Strait game – Dadu

Dadu is a dice game of chance that is played on Waiben and likely originated from Indonesia or the wider Malay Archipelago. Bets can be placed on a number, on the outside Big or Small panels or on a line between the different numbers and Big or Small panels.

The banker is the person who spins the die. The banker spins the die on a saucer and covers the die with a cover while the die is still spinning. Once bets are placed and the die stops spinning, the banker reveals the die results. The banker pays on the number that is facing upwards on the saucer.

The dice are made of dugong bone and the stem through the dice are made of Wongai tree wood which is a local tree often found in the Torres Straits. The cover is half of a polished coconut shell and the handle of the cover is made from the hard base of the coconut frond. The game board is drawn on a canvas sheet which is a similar product used for the sails on the pearling luggers in the Torres Straits. See Figure 2.7 for a sketch of the board and Figure 2.8 for a sketch of the die, cover and saucer.

My Great Dato Tom Loban was born on Banda Neira in Indonesia in 1894. He was there until 1906 and then he was kidnapped while he was out in a canoe fishing. My Great Dato was forced into slavery in the form of indentured labour. Through his time as an indentured labourer, his kidnapper restricted his movements, and made sure never to take my Great Dato when he travelled back to Banda Neira. Great Dato never saw his mother, Tunam, or his sister, Ramina, ever again. Only in his dreams when he slept at night. Great Dato was employed in the pearling industry as a shell grader with the Island Industry Board (IIB) Shell store on Waiben from 1946 to 1969 when he retired because of age and

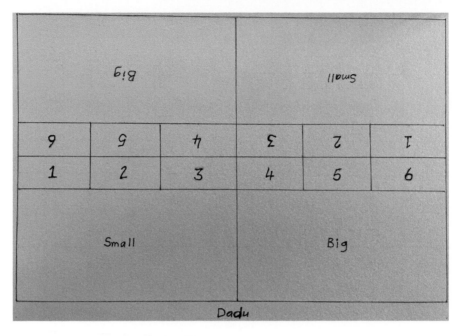

Figure 2.7 The Dadu board layout showing different panels that are mirrored on the other side for players to place bets from different sides [sketch]. This board was sketched by Gehamat Loban.

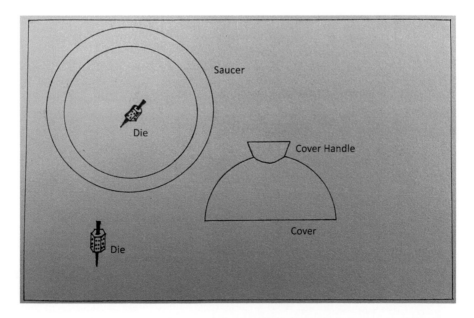

Figure 2.8 Example of the die, cover and saucer used for Dadu [sketch]. Sketch by Gehamat Loban.

Figure 2.9 Great Dato Tom Loban sorting and grading Pearl shells on Waiben [photograph]. Year: Circa 1960.

medical problems. See a photograph of Great Dato at Figure 2.9. I also had other family members involved in the pearling industry including Dato Frank, Dato Ted and even a Pache (uncle) who worked as a pearl shell diver and deckhand before the industry and profession died out in practice. Some of my family also dived for trochus shells as well. Torres Strait Islanders were not only active participants in the pearling industry, but had a reputation as reliable hard workers in a number of industries on the Australian mainland. During times of national conflict, such as World War I (WWI) and World War II (WWII), many Islanders served in the navy, army and air force as well as involvement in building Australia's railway infrastructure.

After the pearling industry

Many Torres Strait Islanders were involved in national service in defence of their community and Australia. My great Dato Tom Loban was involved in the Australian Naval intelligence during WWI with Batcho Mingo, another Indonesian man. They relayed vital information to relate back to the Allied ships. They investigated tracks on Bali, inspected the mountain ranges, and discovered a secret German

Figure 2.10 My father during his time in national service at Enoggera barracks in Brisbane [photograph]. Year: Circa 1972.

wireless plant. Another family member, Dato Ted was enlisted into national service during WWII and was involved in the African desert campaign. He was injured and lost his arm from a German machine gun at close quarters. Dato Frank served in WWII in the American small-ship navy in the Philippines. My father was also involved in national service and was trained as a scout. Just before his battalion was about to be sent to Vietnam, the war was called to an end. See Figure 2.10 for a photograph of my father during national service.

From my perspective, Torres Strait Islanders saw national service as an important contribution and service for the protection of the community and nation with generational involvement. Essentially, the Torres Straits occupies a high strategic position and border between mainland Australia, Papua New Guinea and Indonesia and at times the islands were at the frontline of invading forces. During WWII, islands in the Torres Straits such as Ngurupai were bombed, however, Waiben was spared aerial bombardment by Imperial Japan as it is said that a Japanese Princess is buried on Waiben. I even heard from my father how he and my uncle had spotted the remnants of a Japanese fighter plane in the mangroves around Ngurupai. Nonetheless, national service is a part of the cultural memory of many Torres Strait Islanders, including my own family.

Another significant historical event is the work on the railway tracks with Torres Strait Islanders breaking the world record for laying the longest amount of track in the shortest time.

As Torres Strait Islanders were known for being reliable with a strong work ethic, they were sought after to undertake the arduous work of fettlers, maintaining and changing sleepers and also laying railway tracks in harsh and remote conditions. The Islanders work as a cohesive unit although they may be from different islands. To this day, Torres Strait islanders hold the world recording for laying the greatest number of tracks within a day. My father was part of this record-breaking feat. On 8 May 1968, in the course of laying tracks for 6 months in the Pilbara desert, the Torres Strait Islander crew laid the greatest length of track in one day (Western Australian Museum, 2022). Under scorching sun and extreme heat, the crew laid 7 kilometres of track in 11 hours and 40 minutes which broke the previous record of 4.6 kilometres set in the United States in 1962. The Torres Strait crew comprised of 137 men divided into three teams. Throughout the entire day 896 tons of rail, 11,880 sleepers, 23,760 rail plates, 47,280 rail anchors, 4,280 dog spikes and many tons of track ballast were laid, spiked and anchored (Western Australian Museum, 2022). Laying the entire track from Port Hedland to Mt Newman took 9 months and spanned 400 kilometres. Most Torres Strait Islanders will have family or know somebody who worked on the railway track, and thus this historical event is deeply embedded in the memory of many Torres Strait Islanders. However, perhaps among the most important memories for some Torres Strait Islanders are those histories where we strived for greater autonomy and sovereignty for our communities and way of life.

Community service, advocacy and development

When we think of Torres Strait Islander autonomy and land activism, we may often think of Uncle Eddie Mabo who fought for and started the Native Title land rights claim in Australia (Australian Institute of Aboriginal and Torres Strait Islander Studies, 2022b; Loos & Mabo, 2013). Mer in the Torres Straits is the birthplace of Native Title and the islanders started a movement of Indigenous people throughout Australia to regain ownership and sovereignty over their lands. The High Court decision in regard to Mer Island, dispelled the colonial invention of Terra Nullius and acknowledged Torres Strait Islander's intimate connection and ownership of the land that had always belonged to Torres Strait Islanders. However, I see the Native Title movement as a part of a wider movement by Torres Strait Islanders and Aboriginal peoples to gain greater autonomy and sovereignty over not only over their lands, but also their way of life. In this way, another important part of Torres Strait cultural memory, perhaps the most important, is the service to the community, advocacy for our community and the development of our community for greater autonomy.

Dato Ted (see photograph in Figure 2.11) was a key player and instigator in the effort to secure greater Torres Strait sovereignty including Indigenous representation, building infrastructure, promoting employment on the islands, and shifting

Figure 2.11 Dato Ted Loban [photograph]. Year: Circa 1940.

towards economic independence. For example, Dato Ted founded and directed co-operatives for Waiben and the region that built houses, trained local community members and established new barge services to supply the island. He also helped upgrade the water supply facilities on Ngurupai and build infrastructure (such as a ramp) to receive incoming visitors from other islands. Dato Ted was also an advocate for Indigenous rights in regards to policy changes and education reform. He was involved in organisations such as the National Aboriginal Consultative Committee, School Commission Committee for Aboriginal and Torres Strait Islanders Education, Federal Council for the Advancement of Aborigines and Torres Strait Islanders and many other organisations and initiatives. Dato Ted's sister, Nene Ellie, was also involved in promoting and setting up institutions to promote greater Torres Strait autonomy.

Nene Ellie Gaffney (see photograph in Figure 2.12) was born on 18 August 1932 to Great Dato Tom Loban and Great Nene Gerti Loban (Gaffney, 2015). Nene Ellie was trained as a nurse on mainland Australia and then returned to the islands to better her community. She was crucial in initiating and managing many key organisations in the Torres Strait with most of those organisations existing today such as the Torres Strait Islander Media Association (TSIMA). TSIMA was the

Figure 2.12 Nene Ellie and my father about to go to Port Lihou Island at the back of Muralug [photograph]. Year: Circa 1955.

first media organisation in the Torres Straits and has a very strong female representation. She continued this advocacy for women through the establishment of the Mura Kosker Sorority organisation which both supports the social and health welfare for women in the community and acts as an advocacy vehicle for women's affairs on Waiben (Gaffney, 2015). Through Mura Kosker, she helped establish the aged care facility the Star of the Sea on Waiben in response to the shortage of suitable accommodation (e.g. wheelchair access and handrails) for the aged and disabled residents. Nene Ellie worked to set up the Jumula Dubbins Hostel which was for children coming from the outer islands. These children mostly came to Waiben for schooling and often needed a place to stay. Nene Ellie also represented Torres Strait Islander women at Geneva at the United Nations Indigenous Working Party Conference in 1989 advocating for different community concerns including recognition, education, health, employment and more. Nene Ellie and her work with Mura Kosker Sorority helped establish local institutions and facilities to help many of the most vulnerable in the islands including women, children and the elderly. Her work was to advocate for her community and establish organisations and institutions which we controlled ourselves and allowed greater autonomy.

Figure 2.13 Dato Frank [photograph]. Year: Circa 1943.

Although not as involved in the political negotiation and initiatives to develop the community, my Dato Frank (see photograph in Figure 2.13) was a business-man with a taxi company on Waiben and was respected and helped community wherever he could. He often prioritised community needs over his own business interests and was responsive to community and kinship relationships on the island. Uncle Yen has carried on this tradition of community advocacy and development of the region through his election and appointment as Mayor of the Torres Shire Council. He also runs a ferry service to transport school children between the islands. All these achievements and services for the community contribute to and form a part of the cultural memory of the community, and facilitate greater autonomy and sovereignty over the home islands and the Torres Strait way of life.

Torres Strait cultural memory and sovereignty

These historical time periods and events are held in the memory and identity of many Torres Strait Islanders. The Torres Strait community convey their memories in a variety of art forms. Some in the Torres Strait community express their connection and experience of laying tracks for the railways through songs and dances (Elemo Tapim et al., 2009; Salisbury, 2009). Other Torres Strait artists share their family's and community's stories of the pearl diving industry through artwork, especially through lino prints that transfer traditional Torres Strait wood carvings and etchings, and places them into a paper-based artform (Nona, 2016a; Savage, 2012, 2018). Torres Strait musicians have written and recorded songs about their time at sea and while pearl divining such as Henry 'Seaman' Dan, Cygnet Repu and my own Dato Jerry Lewin with music sung in English, traditional Island languages such as KLY and Malay (Dan, 2019; Lewin, 2003; Repu, 2003). Many Torres Strait families who were also involved in national service express their memories or family's memories through various dance performances, art, contemporary theatrical performances and dance apparel connected to WWII (Mosby, 1998; Nona, 2016b; Queensland Theatre, 2022; Tipoti, 2016). Other art expressions could also be of everyday life and connection to the land, sea and sky. Many of these experiences belong to large sections of the Torres Strait community who have family involved in these historical events. This understanding of history can form a part of what is known as cultural memory.

Torres Strait islands and communities – totems and wind

A totem brings people together and is a representation of a community, island or a group. Rules, structures and assignment of totems will vary from place to place. For example, the totem from my Mabuyag lineage is the dangal (dugong) which is connected to Panay village. From my Boigu line, my totem is the daibau (a yam plant). A community can also be associated with a wind direction. For example, the Panay community on Mabuyag is facing and on the side of the island of Waur (south-east wind) and people from that community will have an affinity with that wind.

According to Assmann (2021), cultural memory can be seen as:

a system of values, artifacts, institutions, and practices that retain the past for the present and the future. It transfers knowledge and supports the emergence and elaboration of distinct identities, because humans define themselves and are defined by their affiliation to one or various cultural groups and traditions
(p. 26).

Cultural memory could be seen as linked to cultural heritage, but certain cultural memories seem to emphasise reflection and construction of memories along with values and meaning of cultural heritage as well as aspects of one's personal life and the connection to wider culture (Apaydin, 2020; Van Dijck, 2004). Cultural memory provides a framework in which we recall the event, importance of events and which events might not be as important (Van Dijck, 2004). However, many of these historical experiences discussed might be seen as more personal cultural memory which stands at the intersection between broader community cultural memory and autobiographical memory, which is more of the history of personal life experiences (Van Dijck, 2004). Memory involves a variety of activities including inscribing or recording, interpreting, narrating, recalling and so on which can be aided by various products that can help stimulate memory such as photographs and videos. We see in the Torres Straits that memory can be captured and then brought back through various art forms such as dance, lino prints and more (Van Dijck, 2004). One's experiences and way of life can be intimately connected with the shared memory of the community and how these are captured and relived through literary and artistic expressions. When we think about Torres Strait culture and particularly history, we can think of each generation adding another layer to the culture and family memory and history. This layering is reflected in Figure 2.14, where each layer of memory adds another component to the culture as a whole.

LAYERS OF TORRES STRAIT CULTURAL MEMORY

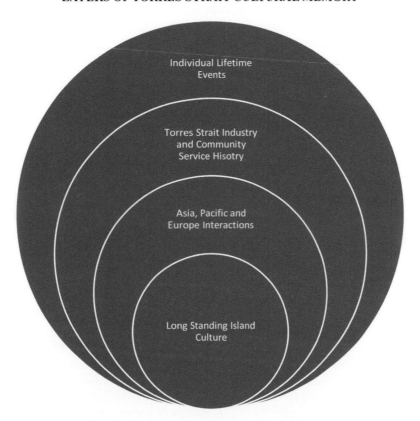

Figure 2.14 Culture is not static and with each generation a new layer can be added to the cultural memory and understanding of the community [graphical diagram].

I consider the formation of our cultural memory and advocacy for sovereignty as deeply intertwined. The Mabo decision was important for Torres Strait Islanders as it meant we could gain ownership and control over our rightful homeland and ensure the self-determination of our people within the islands (Australian Institute of Aboriginal and Torres Strait Islander Studies, 2022b; Loos & Mabo, 2013). I was present at the self-determination for Mabuyag and although I was a child of 11 years at the time, I did not realise the full extent of what was happening. Reflecting back on the determination for Mabuyag, it was an immensely important historical event, and I am proud to have attended and witnessed a step towards gaining greater autonomy. Similarly, as previously discussed, work by Dato Ted, Nene Ellie and the rest of my family is an important part of cultural memory as the community strives for greater autonomy and sovereignty. As a community not a part of a nation-state or with no complete sovereignty, these historical events are important in our cultural memory but obviously not the only part of our cultural memory.

Although I would consider my contribution far less direct and impactful as those achievements by Dato Ted or Nene Gaffney, I saw the epistemological problem of many people, especially within Sydney, Australia, with little awareness let alone knowledge of the Torres Straits. This issue was also prevalent in technology-driven spaces with Torres Strait Islanders minimally represented in digital media. I wanted to educate people, particularly those in the university, on Torres Strait Islander people and our culture. At the time and still today, I enjoy video games and I see Indigenous people are not always represented fully or thoughtfully in the medium. I responded to this issue through creating my virtual reality game about the Torres Straits and using it at the university and other educative settings to teach about the Torres Straits, I feel I have made a very small contribution to furthering the understanding of those who are unaware of the Torres Straits.

Authors like LaPensée et al. (2022) discuss sovereign spaces where nations and communities can reclaim a digital space for their voices and to put forward their perspective of the world. Here, digital spaces can be viewed as extensions of cultural spaces of communities and its related institutions. To better represent ourselves, we need to gain greater control and sovereignty of our own culture and representations in digital mediums and cyberspace. Otherwise, representations are controlled by those outside the community with limited or no experiences of that very same community. In a similar way to Dato Ted and Nene Ellie's perspective of the importance of sovereignty over our own land, community institutions and way of life, it is also important that we reclaim control of our institutions and cultural representations in the digital space.

Shared historical events in the lives of Torres Strait Islanders help to form a cultural memory that binds the community together and over time adds layers to the complex identity of the culture and community. Shared historical experiences and events can be thought of in the framework of cultural memory. These cultural memories are expressed through various arts including lino prints, music, dances, theatre and more recently digital media. For many Torres Strait Islanders, part of this cultural memory and history are the strides for sovereignty and greater autonomy for the community and over our way of life. The creation of digital media and involvement in the depictions of our own culture and community can be seen as a part of claiming of sovereignty and autonomy which extends to a digital space.

Torres Strait cuisine – popular dishes

Dishes from the Torres Straits often draws from the islands for their ingredients. Many of the dish have be brought by or influenced by workers who have come to live in the region. Some of these dishes are listed in the following:

- Sop Sop is a very traditional Torres Strait dish that makes use of the main Torres Straits plant produce of coconuts and edible tubers such a yams and taro as well as pumpkin and sweet potato.
- Semur is chicken-based dish with vermicelli noodles and soy sauce. Although Semur originates from Indonesia, the dish is widespread among the Torres Strait community. Semur dishes tend to vary between families. For example, great Dato Tom Loban was from Banda Neira, a spice island, and in our Semur dish we add nutmeg, cloves and vinegar which are ingredients not necessarily added by other Torres Strait families.
- Sambal is a chilli-based side dish or condiment that often accompanies other dishes. It originates from the Malay Archipelago and was introduced by the Indonesian, Malaysian and Singaporean labourers in the Torres Straits. The dish can be simple and be almost entirely ground chillies or could be a more substantial dish and include blachan, ginger, garlic, onion, vinegar and squid.
- Dinuguan is a pork dish where the meat is cooked in the pig's blood. The dish seems to have originated from the Philippines and was likely introduced to the Torres Straits through Filipino people arriving and working in the Torres Straits.
- Namas (or Namasu) is pickled fish and was likely introduced to the Torres Strait by Japanese pearl shell divers. In preparing Namas, the fish is pickled and cooked via soaking the pieces in vinegar and/or lime juice.

Conclusion

The purpose of this chapter was to provide a contextual understanding of the Torres Straits. This contextualisation is important to better understand the theoretical frameworks and practices through which TSVR was developed. This chapter also provides an example of the types of knowledge you may need to familiarise yourself with before representing different cultures in your video game. This chapter has explored a general overview of the Torres Straits with a focus on geography and history, particularly from the perspective of my own family. First, I have described and illustrated the basic geography of the Torres Straits, the traditional languages of the region and lifestyle to provide a baseline understanding of the Torres Straits. Second, I have discussed my family history and their role in not only historical events shared by a large section of the

Torres Strait Islander community, but also my family's history of advocacy and initiatives for greater Torres Strait autonomy and sovereignty. Third, I have briefly explored how these historical events and personal experiences of my family and community can form a part of the cultural memory of the Torres Strait community and communicated in different art forms. Importantly part of this cultural memory is the advocacy for autonomy of the community and how these efforts continue in a digital space.

The Torres Straits has had a long and vibrant history with each generation adding another layer of history and perspectives to the cultural memory of the community. My family as a part of the community also shares this cultural memory with their involvement in the pearling industry, national service, laying the railroads and, perhaps most importantly, contributing to and advocating for the community. Indeed, part of this cultural memory is the Torres Strait efforts for sovereignty and to regain control of our own community' land, wealth and institutions. I also see my own work around Torres Strait Virtual Reality as a very small part of asserting sovereignty and regaining control of our representations in digital space. The struggle for control over our community's own deeper cultural representations over outside surface depictions of the culture is best exemplified through the Torres Strait concepts of the cultural palm and the Dogai.

References

Apaydin, V. (2020). Introduction: Why cultural memory and heritage? In V. Apaydin (Ed.), Critical *perspectives on cultural memory and heritage*: Construction, *transformation and destruction* (pp. 1–10). UCL Press. https://doi.org/10.2307/j.ctv13xpsfp.6

Assmann, A. (2021). Cultural memory. In Hamburger, A., Hancheva, C., & Volkan, V. D. (Eds.), *Social trauma–an interdisciplinary textbook* (pp. 25–36). Springer.

Australian Institute of Aboriginal and Torres Strait Islander Studies. (2022a). *Australia's First Peoples*. https://aiatsis.gov.au/explore/australias-first-peoples

Australian Institute of Aboriginal and Torres Strait Islander Studies. (2022b). *The Mabo Case*. https://aiatsis.gov.au/explore/mabo-case

Beckett, J. (1990). *Torres Strait Islanders: Custom and colonialism*. Cambridge University Press.

Dan, H. S. (2019). *Forty fathoms*. Perfect Pearls.

David, B., & Ash, J. (2008). What do early European contact-period villages in Torres Strait look like? Archaeological implications. *Memoirs of the Queensland Museum, Culture, 4*(2), 303–324.

Duce, S. J., Parnell, K. E., Smithers, S. G., & McNamara, K. E. (2010). *A synthesis of climate change and coastal science to support adaptation in the communities of Torres Strait*. Reef and Rainforest Research Centre.

Eseli, P., Shnukal, A., & Mitchell, R. (1998). *Eseli's notebook*. University of Queensland.

Gab Titui Cultural Centre. (2022). *Torres Strait*. https://www.gabtitui.gov.au/torres-strait.

Gaffney, E. (1989). *Somebody now: The autobiography of Ellie Gaffney, a woman of Torres Strait*. Aboriginal Studies Press.

Gaffney, E. (2015). *Mura solwata kosker: We saltwater women*. Routledge.

Gur a Baradharaw Kod. (2022). *Our region*. https://www.gbk.org.au/pbcs/.

Hurley, F. (1921). *Pearl diver collecting shells from the beds of Torres Strait, Queensland*. https://nla.gov.au/nla.obj-151335501/view.

Kerr, G. (2010). *The pearl shell divers of Torres Strait: an oral history*. https://www.youtube.com/watch?v=N0rgWxDwJq8

LaPensée, E. A., Laiti, O., & Longboat, M. (2022). Towards sovereign games. *Games and Culture, 17*(3), 328–343.

Lewin, J. (2003). Bada kris. On *Sailing the southeast wind: Maritime music.*

Loos, N., & Mabo, E. K. (2013). *Eddie Koiki Mabo: His life and struggle for land rights.* University of Queensland Press.

Mosby, T. (1998). Chapter 6: Religion is strong because there is nothing necessarily to compensate the spirit. In B. Robinson & T. Mosby (Eds.), *Ilan Pasin (this is our way): Torres Strait art.* Cairns Regional Gallery.

Nona, L. (2016a). *Badhu Habaka.* https://shop.northsite.org.au/products/baduln1

Nona, L. (2016b). *Ngaw Babn ngu Ngayka [from my father to me].* https://www.awm.gov.au/collection/C2140721

Ohshima, G. (1988). Pearl culture and the Islanders' society of the Torres Strait. *GeoJournal, 16*(2), 157–168.

Queensland Government. (2018a). *Mabuiag.* https://www.qld.gov.au/firstnations/cultural-awareness-heritage-arts/community-histories/community-histories-m/community-histories-mabuiag

Queensland Government. (2018b). *Poruma (Coconut Island).* https://www.qld.gov.au/first-nations/cultural-awareness-heritage-arts/community-histories/community-histories-n-p/community-histories-poruma

Queensland Government. (2023). *Queensland globe.* https://qldglobe.information.qld.gov.au/

Queensland Theatre. (2022). *OTHELLO Adapted by Jimi Bani and Jason Klarwein.* https://queenslandtheatre.com.au/plays/othello-22?fbclid=IwAR3xu7sZjpK5f9zu0asonGx-y3NaZQFqN6eaxkeH2O8ko2DmtfObrH7eGfkI

Repu, C. (2003). Khaidhu Baba (Pearling on the Black Swan).On Neuenfeldt, Karl; Pegrum, N: Sailing the southeast wind: Maritime music from Torres Strait. CQ University. Performance. https://hdl.handle.net/10018/32379

Salisbury, D. (2009). Railway Songs: The diaspora of eastern Torres Strait Islander music as a reflection of people, identity and place. In Mackinlay, E., Bartleet, B., and Barney, K. (Eds.), *Musical Islands: Exploring connections between music place and research* (pp. 94–118). Cambridge Scholars Publishing.

Savage, E. (2012). *Au Karem ar Araigi le (Deep Sea Diver).* https://www.nma.gov.au/exhibitions/lag-meta-aus

Savage, S. T. T. (2018). *Pearling days.* https://blacksquarearts.com/shop/pearling-days

Shnukal, A., & Ramsay, G. (2017). Tidal flows: An overview of Torres Strait Islander-Asian contact. In A. Shnukal, G. Ramsay, & Y. Nagata (Eds.), *Navigating Boundaries: The Asian diaspora in Torres Strait.* Pandanus Books.

Singe, J. (1979). *The Torres Strait: People and history.* University of Queensland Press.

State Library of Queensland. (2014). *Pearling luggers of the Torres Strait.* https://www.slq.qld.gov.au/blog/pearling-luggers-torres-strait

Tapim, E., Wailu, V., Captain, P., Tapim, R., Akee, M., Ghee, A., Waitu, L., Tapim, R., Day A., & Gizar, M. (2009). *Eastern Torres Strait Islander railway songs DVD and CD.* https://railwaysongs.blogspot.com/2009/04/torres-strait-islander-railway-songs.html

Tipoti, A. (2016). *Kowbu Gidha Kedha [World war story as its told].* https://www.awm.gov.au/collection/C2140720

Torres Shire Council. (2022a). *About the Torres Straits.* https://www.torres.qld.gov.au/council/about-the-shire/about-the-torres-strait#:~:text=The%20Torres%20Strait%20is%20the,(2011)%20totalled%207490%20people

Torres Shire Council. (2022b). *Local history.* https://www.torres.qld.gov.au/council/about-the-shire/history

Torres Strait Island Regional Council. (2016a). *Arkai (Kubin) – Mua Island.* https://www.tsirc.qld.gov.au/communities/moa-kubin-community

Torres Strait Island Regional Council. (2016b). *Badu.* https://www.tsirc.qld.gov.au/communities/badu

Torres Strait Island Regional Council. (2016c). *Boigu.* https://www.tsirc.qld.gov.au/communities/boigu

Torres Strait Island Regional Council. (2016d). *Dauan.* https://www.tsirc.qld.gov.au/communities/dauan

Torres Strait Island Regional Council. (2016e). *Erub.* https://www.tsirc.qld.gov.au/communities/erub

Torres Strait Island Regional Council. (2016f). *Iama.* https://www.tsirc.qld.gov.au/communities/iama

Torres Strait Island Regional Council. (2016g). *Kirriri.* https://www.tsirc.qld.gov.au/communities/kirriri

Torres Strait Island Regional Council. (2016h). *Mabuiag.* https://www.tsirc.qld.gov.au/communities/mabuiag

Torres Strait Island Regional Council. (2016i). *Masig.* https://www.tsirc.qld.gov.au/communities/masig

Torres Strait Island Regional Council. (2016j). *Mer.* https://www.tsirc.qld.gov.au/communities/mer

Torres Strait Island Regional Council. (2016k). *Our geography.* https://www.tsirc.qld.gov.au/our-communities/our-geography.

Torres Strait Island Regional Council. (2016l). *Poruma.* https://www.tsirc.qld.gov.au/communities/poruma

Torres Strait Island Regional Council. (2016m). *Saibai.* https://www.tsirc.qld.gov.au/communities/saibai

Torres Strait Island Regional Council. (2016n). *Ugar.* https://www.tsirc.qld.gov.au/communities/ugar

Torres Strait Island Regional Council. (2016o). *Warraber.* https://www.tsirc.qld.gov.au/communities/warraber

Torres Strait Island Regional Council. (2016p). *Wug (St Pauls) – Mua.* https://www.tsirc.qld.gov.au/communities/moa-st-pauls-community

Torres Strait Island Regional Council. (2018a). *Badu Island Planning Scheme.* Retrieved from https://www.tsirc.qld.gov.au/sites/default/files/Part%207%20-%20Badu%20Island%20-%20local%20plan%20code.pdf

Torres Strait Island Regional Council. (2018b). *Saibai Island, planning scheme.* http://www.tsirc.qld.gov.au/sites/default/files/Part%207%20-%20Saibai%20Island%20-%20local%20plan%20code.pdf

Torres Strait Regional Authority. (2013*). Profile for management of the habitats and related ecological and cultural resource values of Iama Island.* Prepared by 3D Environmental® for Torres Strait Regional Authority Land …. https://www.tsra.gov.au/__data/assets/pdf_file/0005/4496/Iama_Island_Biodiversity_January_2013.pdf

Torres Strait Regional Authority. (2022). *Our region.* https://www.tsra.gov.au/the-torres-strait/community-profiles

Van Dijck, J. (2004). Mediated memories: Personal cultural memory as object of cultural analysis. *Continuum, 18*(2), 261–277.

Western Australian Museum. (2022). *Breaking a record – Making history.* https://museum.wa.gov.au/explore/online-exhibitions/1968-torres-strait-islander-track-laying-world-record/acknowledgement-c-2#:~:text=On%208%20May%201968%2C%20after,track%20in%20a%20single%20day

Wilson, L. (1993). *Kerkar Lu: Contemporary arterfacts of the Torres Strait Islanders.* Department of Education.

Interlude

Preparing for the Tombstone Opening

Remarks from Gehamat Loban

Figure 2.15 An opened Amai (ground oven) after the cooking process with the top layer
of the tarp cover and almond leaves removed. Almond leaves, banana leaves,
cloth bags and tarps can be used to cover the Amai and keep the heat from the
hot rocks inside the Amai [photograph]. Year: 2022.

DOI: 10.1201/9781003276289-4

The Tombstone Opening signifies the end of the mourning period for a loved one who has passed away. The preparation and planning for this ceremony follow a long-established custom, but this custom may vary from family to family. The Tombstone Opening often takes place 12 months to 2 years after the person has passed or whenever the family can afford to hold the Tombstone Opening. After the relative or friend has passed, we convene a meeting and then nominate and agree on a head person who is charged with planning and coordinating the Tombstone Opening. One of us will need to book a location for the event, such as a hall for the feast. We also ensure to place a notice in the local newspaper and other media to let the community know the date of the Tombstone Opening. This action ensures there is no overlap with other gatherings in the community, but the notice also lets the community know they can attend. We purchase the granite Tombstone head which needs to be engraved along with acquiring the concrete and shell grit for the burial site. We could be planning the entire event for up to 6 to 12 months before the day of the Tombstone Opening. We send invitations to family and friends around the island, on other islands and on the mainland. If we were to invite 50 or more families, we may need to cater for the invitee's other family members who join, such as their children. Therefore, we may be catering for 200 or more people. Sometimes, through word-of-mouth, other people may request to join the event and we will need to cater for them as well.

Several months ahead, we need to plan to acquire the food for the Tombstone Opening. Typically, for the dining setup, we will have a sit-down meal; however, the feast could also be buffet style. For the sit-down meal, we need to arrange for tables and chairs as well as crockery and cutlery for the event. We will need to arrange for family members to dish out the food, share the plates at the event and generally staff the event. There is a great deal of food preparation and cooking involved for the Tombstone Opening. We need to plan for sourcing foodstuffs to be shipped from outside the Torres Straits, such as frozen chickens, vegetables, rice, soy sauce, flour for cakes and more. We can order these items a month or more ahead from Cairns on the mainland, as the local shop on Waiben may not have what we need. In addition, we also plan to obtain local foods such as turtle, dugong, deer and fish. In sourcing local meats, we talk to different people fulfilling various tasks, such as hunting for turtle, dugongs and deer while also catching fish. At the Tombstone Opening, there may even be expectations of having a variety of foods and different kinds of meat at the feast.

When hunting for turtles, dugongs or deer, there is no guarantee that we will be able to catch any just prior to the Tombstone Opening. Therefore, we will need to hunt for the animals one week before the feast. There have been times where we could not locate the animal, so we might have to go again the next day and keep going until we find one. Your responsibilities may depend on your skillset, although this may not always be the case. In regards to the deer, once we find and have it, we need to dress it, dejoint it and possibly debone it to then put the meat into the freezer, ready for the feast. Similar processes will occur with the turtle and dugong.

We have all been given responsibilities, and we need to plan ahead to fulfil them. These responsibilities are allocated at the beginning of the 6 months before the event. Sometimes we encounter obstacles or changes, such as organisers becoming sick, which can arise between the initial planning and the Tombstone Opening. Therefore, we always have iterative and progressive meetings that happen throughout the planning phase. We meet more frequently closer to the event to make sure all the preparations are in order and everyone is fulfilling their part. This process is highly dependent on coordination, working together and fulfilling our obligations. This practice is reciprocal, and other families that are contributing to our family member's Tombstone Opening might ask the same of us in the future. If this person is another family member requesting our support in the future, our obligation is even greater.

Our contribution to the event could include entertainment in the form of dancing, singing and instrument playing. Contributions could also be in the form of material possessions, including lending our boat with fuel for others to use for fishing or hunting the dugongs or turtles. Lending a boat or car can be a valuable contribution as not everyone on the island has a boat or car for transportation. Money or purchased premade food can also be contributions. Several days before the feast, we meet to gather the food and ingredients, take stock and distribute them to the cooks. Depending on the amount of food, we might have different cooking preparations of the same animal. For example, if there are three turtles, we might steam one turtle with soy sauce and lemongrass, barbeque another and cook the last one in an Amai (ground oven). See Figure 2.15 for a photograph of an Amai. We can also cook vegetables and damper in an Amai or separately as different foods cook at different rates.

The night before the Tombstone Opening, we will have a "cut-up night", where we need to debone and cut up the different meats as well as prepare the vegetables and other foods. If there is a large amount of food and we are catering for a larger event, we may need two nights to prepare the food. We can use an open fire, but often we also need to obtain saucepans and other cookware for the cooking in the kitchen. We all keep touching base with the head person. Even informal meetings can occur. For example, if we run into someone in the street, we might talk to them about their situation and how they are progressing with their duties. The procedure as a whole is important as we are all working together through a process as a community for a cultural event.

3   The palm and the Dogai

At the heart of a culture are the community and the people who live and practice the culture. In the Torres Straits, cultural practice was drawn from understandings and knowledge of the surrounding land, sea or sky as well as through community connections. Coconut palms grow abundantly throughout the Torres Straits and are a source of food and a resource used for island life, but the palm is also used as a conceptual framework to understand culture and life. In this context, the coconut palm is physically and deeply rooted and prolific in the surroundings and geography of the Torres Straits. However, the palm tree is also deeply embedded in Torres Strait culture and its metaphysical perspective of the world. Hence, the Torres Strait palm is strongly associated with understandings of deep culture.

This chapter is dedicated to the theoretical explanation and exploration of surface and deep culture and how this discussion intersects with a Torres Strait perspective of culture. First, the chapter begins with a discussion of surface and deep culture which provides a framework for understanding different aspects of culture and cultural representations. Second, the chapter explores how this surface culture and deep culture intersects with the Torres Strait concept of the cultural palm especially in regards to deep culture. Third, the chapter discusses the role of the simulacrum and surface culture, and how these concepts align with the Torres Strait stories of the Dogai. Finally, the chapter suggests there is a continuum from the Dogai which is a simulacrum reflective of only surface culture to the palm which is representative of shifting deep culture. This discussion provides a framework to evaluate video games, and perhaps even other digital media more broadly, in the way they represent different cultures and communities. As described in the previous chapter, cultural portrayals within games can often take on the aesthetics or shallow understandings of a culture without necessarily drawing from deep culture or the context in which they were developed. However, what exactly is deep culture?

Deep culture

Shaules (2007) describes deep culture as the "unconscious meanings, values, norms and hidden assumptions that allow us to interpret our experiences as we interact with other people" (p. 11–12). He suggests that in many intercultural

DOI: 10.1201/9781003276289-5

contexts deep culture is not obvious or even well understood by an outsider. Shaules (2007) uses the example of a foreign visitor to Thailand encountering significant cultural difference when observing monks with begging bowls. As a visitor, this experience is not a Thai experience, rather it is a foreigner's experience in Thailand. He suggests that this practice might seem highly spiritual and sacred; however, it is actually an everyday routine for many Thai people. Shaules' understanding of deep culture emphasises a hidden aspect that is not immediately apparent and suggests our experiences of other cultures are mostly our cultural interpretation of the experience.

Terreni and McCallum (2003) in their discussion of deep culture use the idea of a cultural iceberg. The iceberg signposts that cultural practices can be divided into surface culture and deep culture. Surface culture may include practices such as art, dancing, dress, cooking and so on and are recognised through primary awareness. However, below the surface there are deep practices that are primarily outside of awareness of the individual such as relationships to nature, social interactions, roles in relation to age, sex, class, occupation and kinship. Deep cultural practices tend to be more internalised and exist and operate at a more unconscious level within an individual. These hidden practices exist below the surface of the iceberg and are at a deeper level of abstraction, and include values, thought patterns and some beliefs (Weaver, 2000). In another example, surface and deep culture is visualised as a tree (Holtzman & Sharpe, 2014). In this tree, surface culture, i.e. the branches, are quite visible and can take the form of food, clothing, language, music, dance and material culture. Whereas the roots representing deep culture are more hidden in the form of values, beliefs and customs and can be seen in the form of child-rearing, courtship and marriage practices, and treatment of elders. In these explanations, we see the visually recognisable and apparent surface culture compared to the deep culture which can often provide context and meaning to surface culture.

Building on the iceberg concept, Bent (2017) discusses a similar notion of an iceberg with three layers. The surface culture represents observable behaviours while the intermediate culture may be symbols and meanings which are important to the society. Deep culture is seen to be the traditions, beliefs and values of a society. Bent (2017) also considers the difficulty of teaching deep-level culture in a classroom. Surface-level culture, clothing, food dishes and festivals can be shown through physical props or through pictures. These examples can also be read about in books or viewed on visual media. However, deep aspects of culture are much harder to demonstrate or communicate. For this reason, I also emphasise cultural immersion and Learning from Country which I discuss later in the book in Chapter 6 (Harrison & Skrebneva, 2020). Deep culture typically needs to be discussed or experienced firsthand. However, even then, these experiences are often filtered through the recipients own cultural lens with the recipient often substituting their own understandings with the intended meaning from the culture.

In another approach by Herron et al. (2000), culture can be understood as a 'big C' and 'little c'. 'Little c' refers to cultural practices and 'big C' refers to cultural products. In a similar perspective, 'Big C' can refer to formal culture and include knowledge of great figures in history, politics and products of literature, fine arts and science which could be found in books (Bell, 2020). 'Little c' might refer to daily living and include elements such as food, tools, clothing and behavioural patterns. Other authors (Hall, 1989; van den Hoven, 2006) suggest that the 'big C' culture can be seen as visible aspects, easy to read and study and are interesting, colourful, exciting and even shocking. On the other hand 'small c' culture is an invisible (hidden) aspect of culture that is hard to discover as it influences how people think and act, but 'small c' culture is best used to understand the elements of other cultures (Hall, 1989; van den Hoven, 2006). Thus, similar to surface and deep culture, there is a division between the 'big C' cultural aspects which are the most observable and formal aspects of culture and the 'little c' or 'small c' culture which are hidden and informal but often fundamentally a deeper reflection of the culture and way of life.

In other research, Hall (1959) argues that culture exists within a context with cultures existing on a continuum from high context to low context cultures. Many cultures tend to be either more high or more low context. However, cultures are not exclusively high or low context, but rather vary on a continuum. In this theory, high-context cultures typically require understanding of the context and rules which are not always clear (Hall, 1989). Conversely, in low-context cultures, rules are explained and verbalised and need to be explicit. In a practical sense, for example, language students of high-context cultures might need to learn what is acceptable and expected behaviour within certain cultural contexts in order to effectively communicate (Fong & DeWitt, 2019). In many high-context cultures, it may not be apparent that a particular cultural practice is important and it may be assumed to be the norm. To this end, even an individual can be unaware of their own cultural values and thought patterns (Weaver, 2000). Understanding one's own hidden culture is important because it is an awareness of our own biases and our ability to avoid judgements (Hall, 1989). Therefore, we do not necessarily notice our own cultural perspective and programming, let alone know how others perceive what we say and do. These cultural perspectives and programming could be seen as part of the less accessible and discernible deep culture.

In essence, there is a general recognition of deep and surface-level culture. Surface culture tends to be visible and could include food, clothing, music and other material culture. Some authors suggest that these surface-level elements might be easier to teach through books and other less experiential pedagogy. On the other hand, deep culture is less apparent and represents deeper understandings, traditions, values, beliefs and customs of the community. Deep culture seems to be harder to access through theoretical and non-experiential teachings. Instead, experience is best used to access deep culture. These understandings are represented in Figure 3.1. in the form of an iceberg. Both are reflections of culture and are interlinked, but certainly the deep culture is more important to fully understand a culture in a meaningful way. The Torres Strait cultural palm tree shares some similarities to the discussed perspectives on deep culture.

CULTURAL ICEBERG

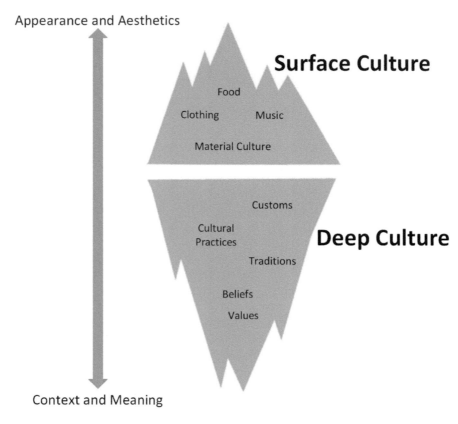

Appearance and Aesthetics

Context and Meaning

Figure 3.1 The cultural iceberg of surface and deep culture shows a continuum from appearance and aesthetics of a culture to deeper understanding of the culture which emphasises the context and meaning in which cultural practices and materials are developed [graphical diagram].

Cultural palm tree

In the Torres Straits, coconut palms are central to island life. All sorts of foods or ingredients can come from the coconut palm including coconut flesh, coconut water, coconut milk, coconut oil and desiccated coconut. Other parts of the coconut palm can also be used to create a range of woven objects which have multiple uses including mats, bags, hats, house parts, and containers. Brooms are made from palm fronds, while the coconut husk can be used as an insect repellent. Palm fronds may also be used to wrap food, cook food and serve food. Because of the palm's centrality to island life, the coconut palm is also often used by Torres Strait Islanders to explain deep cultural knowledge and cultural shifts throughout time.

Torres Strait item – woven island mats

Mats are commonly made from palm fronds (from Coconut palms) or pandanas leaves (from the Screw palms) and are central to the culture in the Torres Straits. Children are born on mats, you can sleep on mats, you can sit down on the mats and mats are also placed with the deceased community members when they are buried. Hence, mats are seen as not only a practical item to use but also have a symbolic place for many Torres Strait Islanders. Given the importance of mats, weaving is a valuable skill. See Figure 3.2. for a photograph of a typical palm weaving.

The Torres Strait cultural palm can have different meanings for different people. For some Islanders, the palm is used to represent knowledge sharing being passed on through the generations (Harrison & Sellwood, 2016; Whap, 2001). However, for my family and I, the Torres Strait cultural palm is seen as a way to understand and represent culture, and how it can shift over time. In this concept of the

Figure 3.2 Close-up of typical weaving for Island mats made from palm fronds [photograph].

cultural palm, the roots represent deeply embedded and long-standing traditions, beliefs, customs, values, and cultural practices and understandings. These deeply embedded cultural elements are interlinked, mediated and transformed through the individual's own interpretation which is depicted as the palm's trunk. At the trunk level, the individual's own learnings, research and interpretations are combined with the original deep culture through a synergistic process. Thereafter, new expressions and outputs of culture are represented as fronds that grow from the top of the palm. These expressions and outputs can be new forms of culture such as different takes on Torres Strait art, music or media. The trunk mediates, supports and interlinks the roots to the fronds. In some versions of the cultural palm, the canopy area produces coconuts that drop off the palm to create new palms. The dropped coconut seeds become new palms that develop deep roots. The next generation of palms symbolise newly produced Torres Strait culture becoming a new form of deep culture through the generations. All aspects of the palm are a representation of culture and its shifting nature. See Figure 3.3 for a visual depiction of the Torres Strait cultural palm.

The new cultural outputs and expressions signified by fronds could be different takes on dance, songs, art and media. However, these new cultural outputs can even be smaller shifts in cultural practices. For example, in the Torres Straits, because it is a collection of islands, we often travel to other islands to visit families or friends. When your visiting guest arrives at your island, you will walk out into the water to greet them in their dinghy (small boat), grab the dinghy and help bring their dinghy onto shore where the visitors can disembark. When the person greeting the visitor walks out into the ocean, they may walk out until the water reaches their knees or waist, wherever they feel comfortable. However, they do walk out into the water to greet them and bring them in which is symbolic of bring visitors into your home. Similarly, when we farewell visitors or family, we help drag the dinghy into the water and walk out into the water again to see them off. This practice can be seen as greeting and welcoming those who are coming to the island, letting them know it is alright to visit and that you are looking after them while they are a guest at your place as well as farewelling them as they depart.

This deep connection to a place does not mean that culture is expressed only through connection to the surroundings, rather it travels with the people wherever they may go, and cultural practices are adapted to where they live. My family now lives in suburban Brisbane, but our cultural practices continue albeit differing slightly. In the same way, my family will often wait for guests to arrive and once we see guests arrive in their car, we will go outside to meet them. We would exit the house go down the stairs, along the footpath, down the driveway and then either meet the guests at the gate or even meet them on the road. We will bring the guests in while talking to them. Similarly, when the guests depart, we accompany them to the car on the road while talking, helping them into the car and then wave to them as they drive off. For me, this is starkly different from some other cultures where you may meet and greet a visitor at the door of the house and bid you farewell at the door of the house. In this Torres Strait approach, we can see that the cultural practices of greeting and send-offs can remain consistent even when not

Figure 3.3 Torres Strait cultural palm shows the roots representing deep culture, the trunk symbolising the person mediating the creation of new cultural outputs and the fronds represent the new cultural outputs and expressions [painting]. Original illustration by Xia Hua.

living on your island place as the practice is drawing from deep existing cultural practices.

The Torres Strait cultural palm shows that culture changes through new outputs that are drawn from deep culture. These new outputs are also interlinked and mediated by the individual's experiences and understandings. The cultural palm differs from surface and deep culture as the palm is also an explanation for how culture changes and produces new outputs. However, these new outputs are always from a place of deep culture and understanding. In opposition to the concepts of deep culture and the palm, are cultural representations of primarily the appearance and aesthetic with only a limited reflection of culture. However, if one only recognises the surface-level representation, new outputs can have limited and distorted deeper meanings of culture. This notion is also represented through the concepts of the Dogai and the simulacrum (Baudrillard, 1994).

The simulacrum

As we have seen in Chapter 1, culture can be represented through literature, art media and other representations we encounter in life. Some of these depictions can be misrepresentations of a culture or community. However, not all literary, art or media representations are direct representations of their real-life equivalents. Through time, reproductions of an original representation can morph into a representation of a representation of an original. These representations can be second-hand and third-hand interpretations of the real-equivalent and can often transform or become warped in their depictions. Baudrillard (1994) described this phenomenon as the simulacrum. A simulacrum could be described as a representation of a representation and so on that no longer represents the original (Baudrillard, 1994). A simulacrum could also be a representation that had no meaningful connection to an original to begin with. Baudrillard (1994) has a theory of different stages ranging from believable and near-truthful copies to those of pure simulacrum with no relation to the original. The abundance of various simulacrums we encounter today can induce what is called hyperreality. In this state, one cannot distinguish between actual reality and a copy (Baudrillard, 1994). This concept is even further confounded in a gaming context. For example, a player interprets a game which is the game designer's interpretation of a book on culture which is an anthropologist's interpretation of a cultural they may have experienced and interpreted. Each representation is a re-representation of the one before it and obscures the culture from its original state in both the representation inside and outside the minds of the audience. These simulacrums encountered everyday can invoke a hyperreality where you are unable to tell what is real and what is a copy, or a copy of a copy and so on.

A simulacrum also needs to be distinguished from verisimilitude, which is the feeling or appearance of an original representation. Apperley (2013) argues that some historical games can provide a verisimilitude, that is the feeling of or appearance of history, particularly in a video game context. Penix-Tadsen (2016) also suggests that verisimilitude is an abstraction of reality that is then represented in games, so that it is not an exact replication of real life, but enough that it feels believable. In the same way, some games are given the appearance of belonging to a culture even if they are not an exact representation of the original. The verisimilitude of culture or history could be suitable for many games depending on who is creating the game content and the engagement the game has with the culture or history.

The simulacrum and verisimilitude are not necessarily inherently intentionally deceitful or harmful representations or communications on their own. In some cases, a simulacrum may occur as a natural re-representation of an original over-time. On the other hand, Verisimilitude, in some cases, is implemented to present history or culture which might not be practicable within the game, but is useful for communicating large and complex concepts through a game. For example, some building architecture within a game might not match the exact detail of a building in real life, but it might feel and appear real enough to provide a historical feeling of time that will add to a game trying to invoke history in their storyline, such as in Assassins Creed II with the depictions of historical buildings (Dow, 2013). In this instance, these historical representations may not be misrepresentations, instead they stand for abstracted representations of the original. However, these are more related to creative design choices and shortcuts as opposed to the issue of cultural representation and misrepresentation, but are still relevant to the domain of video games and game design.

Nonetheless, the main concept of the simulacrum relevant here is that some cultural depictions are received and established in the mind of the audience that are not true in a meaningful sense. In this way, deep representations of the culture are substituted for representations that do not have a meaningful or genuine connection to the culture or community. However, the issue here is not the abstraction or changes from the real-life representation or new aesthetic representations of culture as the Torres Strait cultural palm accounts for these changes. Instead, it is how this new representation is developed, who is involved in the design process and how the wider public perceives the representations. As pointed out by Said (1978), some representations are distorted and exaggerated to begin with and do not come from the place of deep culture. Thus, subsequent representations of the original exaggerated misinterpretation stray further from any real meaning to the culture and transforms into a different representation. While some cultural representations might represent the surface culture and the aesthetics, they do not represent deep culture or the meaning and context below the surface. However, while representations of surface-level cultural might invoke a form of hyperreality for those not familiar with the deep culture, those from the community can often distinguish between representations of merely surface culture and those with deeper connections. This phenomenon is best represented through the Torres Strait story figure of the Dogai.

The Dogai

In the Torres Straits, stories are often intimately connected to the land, sea and sky. Parts of the stories relate or serve as origin stories about how the surroundings came to be. Stories also frequently carry important morals or can be used to better understand local knowledge related to the landscape and sea such as the story of Gelam which can be used to better understand the geography and plants of the islands. Different stories can be told on different islands, or the same story may be told between the islands but may have some differences and similarities. As such, there are many stories with various characters told within the Torres Strait community. In one story, the giant Wawa enjoys eating turtles and commands various sinister birds to carry out his will. In another story, Pontianak, originating from the Malay Archipelago, lives in Frangipani trees and waits at night to attack and seize young men (Nicholas & Kline, 2010). However, perhaps one of the most retold and universally known story characters in the Torres Straits is the Dogai. The Dogai is a female spirit who typically has malevolent intentions in her various interactions with Islanders (Gela, 1993; Lawrie, 1970). For example, in the story of Dogai Metakurab, after being disturbed from her slumber, she terrorises the village of Tuam on Boigu. Dogai Metakurab is often followed by swarms of sandflies, mosquitoes, and giant butterflies (Lawrie, 1970). In another story, the Dogai in *Gelam: The Man from Moa* (Gela, 1993), disguises herself with seaweed and attacks a village on Moa Island hunting for people. In multiple stories she has a vast number of powers, from being aided by insects to reassembling severed parts of her body to sinking into and concealing herself in the ground (Lawrie, 1970). However, one of the Dogai's most renowned abilities is to disguise and transform herself. See Figure 3.4 for an illustration of the shapeshifting Dogai.

Torres Strait story – Gelam

Gelam is a cultural hero and is universally known throughout the Torres Straits. He is said to have travelled on a dugong from Moa across the Torres Straits stopping at various islands along the way. He arrived and stayed on Mer and now there is an eye-catching hill in the shape of a dugong on the island. Gelam does not feature in TSVR, but another character from his story, Kupas, does feature in the game.

The extent of the Dogai's shapeshifting abilities can range from natural camouflage with the environment to complete transformations into other animals or even into different people. This power to take on other identities is best exemplified through the story of Giz the Dogai (Lawrie, 1970). In this story, Giz longs to be with an expert hunter named Kaudab, who Giz observes from afar. However, Kaudab already has a wife named Bakar and Giz grows jealous and plans to kidnap Bakar. After setting and springing a trap, Giz banishes Bakar to an underground path which Bakar follows to the end in the story. Meanwhile, Giz transforms to take on the appearance of Bakar and takes her place as Kaudab's wife. Giz tries to please Kaubad by cooking for him. However, she does not know how to handle the cookware such as tongs, and Giz uses her hands to handle foods from hot stones.

Figure 3.4 The Dogai [painting]. Illustration by Xia Hua.

She burns herself and speaks in a distorted version of island language. Kaudab realises then that the being posing as Bakar is in fact a Dogai.

In this story, the fact that Dogais can only physically transform is their undoing. While Dogais can take forms of others to disguise themselves in Island society, Dogais have no knowledge of the nuances of how to act or operate in Islander society and are often exposed through their give aways such as lack of knowledge around cooking and language. The lack of intimate understanding about the context and society means that in the case of Giz, she is soon discovered by Kaudab to be an imposter. This story exemplifies how something can take the shape of another, but fundamentally it misrepresents and lacks any of the deep understandings or nuances of what it is trying to represent. The representation is only superficial and does not have meaningful knowledge of the context. The Dogai's representation therefore remains at a surface-level understanding because that is all she knows, and she reproduces that representation in her imitation.

In a similar vein, some games may attempt to capture and represent various cultures in-game often based on shallow, limited or no understandings about the culture. Certainly, some aspects of the cultural representation may have some truth in the aesthetic or surface-level representation. In the story of Giz, her observation of Islander society helped her understand familial and matrilineal connections, so she could replace Bakar to get close to Kaudab and become his wife. Giz's observation of the fire was also important in the creation of meals. However, because she had only relied on what she saw from a distance, she lacked any meaningful or deep understanding of Islander society or societal practices. She did not have the intimate experience within the society or community. In a similar way, games designed around only outside observation or second-hand experience of the culture will miss the nuances and likely the deeper meaning of the culture. In fact, this lack of understanding or misunderstanding may be multiplied depending on how many interpretations of the culture has occurred in relation to the initial cultural understanding (e.g. interpretation of culture then an interpretation of an interpretation of the culture). Again, these misrepresentations could be unintentional or well-intended, but nonetheless they still occur and are noticed by the communities being represented. Therefore, from the cultural palm to the Dogai, we can see a continuum from deep culture to surface culture.

The palm and the Dogai

As shown in Figure 3.5, the Dogai end of the continuum highlights a shallow cultural simulacrum in-game which the community sees as an imposter with no nuanced or deep understanding of the culture. While at the cultural palm end, the figure highlights a game which has been embedded in and draws from deep understandings and knowledges in the community to create a game that is not only culturally sound but can communicate community perspectives in-game. The figure highlights that this movement between the Dogai and the cultural palm is not binary but rather a continuum. When designers move towards a deeper reflection of the community through different practices and engagement with the community, they can better generate a more meaningful cultural gaming experience. See Figure 3.5 for a depiction of the cultural palm-Dogai continuum.

The palm and the Dogai exemplifies the kind of cultural representations that can be seen in video games and the relationship those cultures and communities have with those in-game representations. In-game depictions of culture that are Dogai

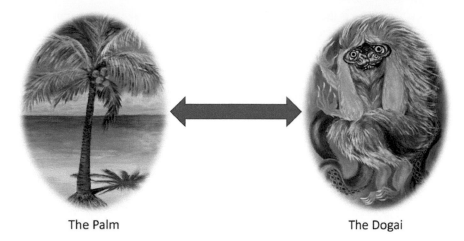

The Palm   The Dogai

Figure 3.5 The palm-Dogai continuum shows a range from deep-level cultural representations to the surface-level cultural representations. The palm stands for context
and meaning of the cultural representations while the Dogai is representative of
the aesthetics and limited knowledge [paintings and graphical diagram].

like in nature, such depictions may not necessarily be the intentional creation of
designers. Most game designer would likely want to create sound and genuine
cultural depictions that do not elicit criticism from the communities represented in
these games. Yet, many games still encounter challenges when depicting various
cultures and communities in respectful and deep ways. Therefore, throughout the
game design and development process cultural considerations and practices need
to be reflected on and integrated into the game design to shift towards the palm
and away from Dogaism (a Dogai-like product). By placing culture as an essential
component of the product development, a project can take on a culturally centred
approach where by culture strongly shapes the game design and decision-making
process.

Conclusion

Collectively, deep culture provides the context and meaning of the culture while
surface culture is representative of the aesthetics, appearance and a limited portrayal of the culture. Deep culture and surface culture can also be seen in the representations of the Torres Strait cultural palm and the Dogai. The palm represents
deep culture and functions in a way where the roots signify long-standing culture
and can include traditions, customs and cultural practices and understandings. The
palm trunk represents the individual who is mediating the culture and the fronds
represent new cultural outputs such as dance, art, music and so on. New cultural
outputs can be produced by drawing from the roots which are interlinked to and
mediated through the trunk to produce new fronds. The fronds are not an exact copy
of the roots, but they come from the same place and understanding. In opposition

to the cultural palm is the Dogai who is a shapeshifter and takes on the appearance, aesthetics and shallow representation of another with no deep understanding of the original.

In the context of video games and game design, designers may not have much experience or knowledge with the culture they are representing in-game and therefore create games based on limited understandings that depict surface culture in-game. While these games might appear to be of the culture, the games may lean towards Dogaism and not be representative of deep culture. This process may be unintentional and well intentioned, but the result is the same, nonetheless. The community of the depicted culture can typically recognise that the game shifts towards Dogaism because there are tells that only those with intimate experience with the community would recognise. In contrast, games that align with the cultural palm philosophy draw from deep culture interlinked and mediated by the designer to create a new cultural product or representations in-game. The depiction in-game or the medium itself does not have to be an exact replica of the culture before it; however, the new cultural game production or depiction comes from a place of deep experience and understanding of the culture. That is video games or in-game representations are centrally derived from the community itself. The next chapter will show how my team and I tried to place culture at the centre of the game design process, integrate cultural considerations and practices into the design, and the challenges we encountered while designing Torres Strait Virtual Reality.

Reference

Apperley, T. (2013). Modding the Historians' code: Historical verisimilitude and the counterfactual imagination. In M. W. Kapell & A. B. Elliott (Eds.), *Playing with the past: Digital games and the simulation of history* (pp. 185–198). Bloomsbury Academic. http://dx.doi.org/10.5040/9781628928259.ch-012

Baudrillard, J. (1994). *Simulacra and simulation*. University of Michigan press.

Bell, T. R. (2020). Integrating big C and little C culture into novice-level university German curriculum. In Burke, B. (Ed), *Room for All at the Table* (pp. 95–123).

Bent, R. (2017). How deep should we go? The role of deep culture in the EFL classroom. 活水論文集. 文学部編= *The Kwassui review*, 図書・学術活動委員会 編(60), 15–25.

Dow, D. N. (2013). Historical veneers: Anachronism, simulation, and art history in Assassin's Creed II. In M. W. Kapell & A. B. R. Elliott (Eds.), *Playing with the past: Digital games and the simulation of history*. Bloomsbury.

Fong, C. S., & DeWitt, D. (2019). Developing intercultural communicative competence: Formative assessment tools for mandarin as a foreign language. *Malaysian Journal of Learning and Instruction*, *16*(2), 97–123.

Gela, A. A. (1993). *Gelam the man from Moa: A legend of the people of the Torres Strait Islands*. Magabala Books.

Hall, E. T. (1959). *The silent language* (Vol. 948). Anchor books.

Hall, E. T. (1989). *Beyond culture*. Anchor.

Harrison, N., & Skrebneva, I. (2020). Country as pedagogical: Enacting an Australian foundation for culturally responsive pedagogy. *Journal of Curriculum Studies*, *52*(1), 15–26.

Harrison, N. E., & Sellwood, J. (2016). *Learning and teaching in Aboriginal and Torres Strait Islander education*. Oxford University Press South Melbourne.

Herron, C., Dubreil, S., Cole, S. P., & Corrie, C. (2000). Using instructional video to teach culture to beginning foreign language students. *Calico Journal*, 395–429.

Holtzman, L., & Sharpe, L. (2014). *Media messages: What film, television, and popular music teach us about race, class, gender, and sexual orientation*. Routledge.

Lawrie, M. (1970). *Myths and legends of Torres Strait*. University of Queensland Press.

Nicholas, C. L., & Kline, K. N. (2010). Cerita Pontianak: Cultural contradictions and patriarchy in a Malay ghost story. *Storytelling, Self, Society*, 6(3), 194–211.

Penix-Tadsen, P. (2016). *Cultural code: Video games and Latin America*. MIT press.

Said, E. (1978). *Orientalism*. Routledge.

Shaules, J. (2007). *Deep culture: The hidden challenges of global living* (Vol. 16). Multilingual matters.

Terreni, L., & McCallum, J. (2003). Providing culturally competent care in early childhood services in New Zealand. Part 1: Considering culture [and] Part 2: Developing dialog [and] Part 3: Parents' experiences of different early childhood pedagogies.

van den Hoven, M. (2006). Big C and small C: Culture as a tree. *The English Connection*, 16.

Weaver, G. R. (2000). Contrasting and comparing cultures. *Culture, Communication and Conflict: Readings in Intercultural Relations* (2nd ed. Revised, pp. 72–77). Simon & Schuster.

Whap, G. (2001). A Torres Strait Islander perspective on the concept of Indigenous knowledge. *The Australian Journal of Indigenous Education*, 29(2), 22–29. http://citeseerx.ist. psu.edu/viewdoc/download?doi=10.1.1.512.305&rep=rep1&type=pdf

4 Culturally centred game design

To recap the key argument in the book to this point. I have briefly explored how in the past and today, media have frequently represented various cultures and communities often without their input. This practice has continued in video games and game design. For many communities, there are continued efforts to regain sovereignty over their lives and these efforts can be seen as extending into the cultural representations in the digital space. This issue of representation is captured through the concept of the Dogai that can reflect the aesthetics or limited understanding of the culture in-game, but does not represent any deep or meaningful aspects. In contrast to Dogaism is the Torres Strait cultural palm. The palm illustrates cultural shifts over time, but also how deep culture can be used to inform the creation of new cultural products that are still faithful to the context and meaning of the culture. These new cultural outputs are not exact replicas of previous deep cultural representations. However, throughout the creation process, deep culture becomes a centralised part of the production of the new cultural output.

This chapter outlines the development and design process of Torres Strait Virtual Reality (TSVR) which I consider a new palm frond and a new cultural product informed by deep culture. The game design of TSVR placed culture at the centre of the decision-making process that guided the project team. This chapter explores different aspects of the game design process of TSVR and how cultural considerations and practices are incorporated into the game design and decision-making process. From the art and asset choices to the gameplay to the very premise of the game, cultural considerations and practices informed the various aspects of the game design to best represent Torres Strait culture.

Unintentionally, the TSVR project followed the Critical Indigenous Research Methodologies (CIRM) approach by Brayboy et al. (2012). CIRM provides a framework around which to engage Indigenous communities in research. Although CIRM originates from the perspective of other Indigenous communities, I found the four guiding principles aligned with many aspects of how I approached game design from a Torres Strait Islander perspective. The CIRM provides a respectful framework for engaging in research with Indigenous communities, however, this framework can also be applied to the game design process involving cultural representations and community engagement. Here, CIRM provides an excellent framework for cultural representations in games centred around community

DOI: 10.1201/9781003276289-6

involvement and thoughtful game design. CIRM emphasises four key elements: relationality, responsibility, respect and reciprocity. Collectively, TSVR project's cultural practices and considerations unintentionally aligned with these elements. An important part of CIRM are relationships, particularly for those involved in the project. In TSVR project, this started with a culturally connected project team.

Critical Indigenous Research Methodologies – relationality

Relationality suggests that knowledge is relational and it is not necessarily owned by, or the product of any one individual, but rather shared between communities and groups of people (Brayboy et al., 2012). In a game design example, the representation of culture in-game is a representation of knowledge, but the process to construct such knowledge should be relational. Therefore, community involvement is very important in the design of the game. In another example, some knowledge is relational, but only within the community and is typically not shared outside the community. Therefore, you might need to consult with the community about the appropriateness of which knowledges can be represented in-game.

Critical Indigenous Research Methodologies – responsibility

Responsibility emphasises a responsibility on the part of the researcher to the community and the need to be considerate of community participation and cultural protocols when engaging with a community or culture (Brayboy et al., 2012). In a game design example, you might be responsible for fulfilling certain cultural protocols and obligations during the community engagement in the game design process. In another example, you might be responsible for the representations you depict in the game and therefore have a duty of care towards the community.

Critical Indigenous Research Methodologies – respect

Respect asserts that the relationship, interactions and the project as a whole are respectful to all parties, especially the community and culture which are the focus of the project (Brayboy et al., 2012). In a game design example, you might ask if your artistic representations or assets in-game are respectful? Check with the community, and if not, are there other art assets or even alternative methods (e.g. sound or game mechanics) that can be used to communicate the idea in a different way?

Critical Indigenous Research Methodologies – reciprocity

Reciprocity focuses on building relationships that are reciprocal, and relationships that are genuine and mutually beneficial (Brayboy et al., 2012). Relationships that are focused on the needs of one individual or one group (usually from outside the community) are not reciprocal relationships. A relationship that is exploitive or relationships that are transactional without any intent of long-term partnerships also stand in opposition to reciprocity. In a game design example, while working with the community, you might ask are the relationships you are forming genuine and non-transactional? Are you also fairly compensating the community for their contributions to the project?

The project team

The size of the TSVR project team was relatively small. The team included myself as the project lead, main designer and developer, and my father, a Torres Strait Elder, who strongly shaped and supported the project. I was assisted by two undergraduate media students with training in Unreal Engine 4 as well as learning Maya on the job. Both of the undergraduate students were not Torres Strait Islanders. The project was also managed by different project managers from the university over the life of the project. The project managers assisted with the finances and administrative side of the project.

As a Torres Strait Islander, I had knowledge about and experiences of many cultural aspects depicted in-game and I was able to speak with certainty and a degree of authority. However, my approach was supported by the Torres Strait Elder who was a cultural knowledge holder. The familial Elder was central to the team, and the game design and direction were strongly influenced by him. He played a significant role in deciding both major and minor decisions related to the cultural representations and the overall design of TSVR. By receiving and acting on feedback from the Elder and the wider community (discussed in Chapter 5), we were engaging in a relational approach to game design (Brayboy et al., 2012). We were also upholding respect of the community by valuing their contributions through the community participation process. While there were technical and resource constraints, most of the Elder's recommendations and many of the community's suggestions were built into the game.

Torres Strait Virtual Reality storyline and premise: The Tombstone Opening

In the beginning of the game design process, there was brainstorming between the Elder and myself about possible storylines for the game. Many ideas were floated during our initial brainstorming session for the game's premise. However, we settled on an idea quite early that we wanted the game to not only be distinctly Torres Strait in the setting, but also have a storyline that strongly related to the Torres Straits. We thought the game's story told through processes and interactions in VR fitted well with the cultural protocols required for cultural ceremonies and events. I noted the cultural learning through processes shared similarities to the premise of the game-based learning theory of Procedural Rhetoric (Bogost, 2007). Just as an audience can learn through verbal rhetoric by listening to a speaker or through the visual rhetoric by viewing images, Procedural Rhetoric is the power to communicate information or stories through the engagement with processes such as those in video games. This approach to learning through processes and procedures matched well with the cultural protocols and processes that need to be followed and engaged with for an event or ceremony in Torres Strait culture. Initially, we had considered basing the premise of TSVR around the Torres Strait Shaving ceremony; however, we decided to depict the lead up to a Tombstone Opening instead as we had more collective experience and knowledge about the Tombstone Opening. Furthermore, we believed the technical depiction of the shaving ceremony would be difficult to capture compared to our current representation of the Tombstone Opening.

Torres Strait cultural event – shaving ceremony

Originally, we had built the game around a shaving ceremony, which is the coming-of-age event for young men. In this ceremony, a young man will have his first shave. In traditional Torres Strait customs, young men typically do not shave until around the age of 17 or 18 or whenever it is possible to arrange the event. The event is typically overseen and directed by the mother's brother (or brother-in-law to the father) of the son. There are specific protocols associated with the shaving ceremony in addition to other event components such as a feast, dancing, singing and other preparatory aspects.

For many Torres Strait Islanders, the Tombstone Opening is central to island life and is a custom shared among most if not all the Island communities in the Torres Straits and on the mainland. It is often seen as a connection to the past. There is a strong belief that the Tombstone Opening originates from Malay and Islamic custom as the timings and practices are similar to Malay cultural customs and religious practices. For many Islanders with Malay connections, the Tombstone Opening and Malay burial practices are one and the same. The ceremony was often combined with Islander artefacts which were placed on the Tombstone (Elu, 2004). The syncretic nature of Torres Strait culture has resulted from intermarriages and cultural exchange between different communities. Hence different customs and protocols are brought into Torres Strait cultural practice.

In more current contexts, the Tombstone Opening combines Islamic and Christian burial practices with Islander artefacts and traditions and is practiced by many Torres Strait Islanders regardless of cultural background or religious beliefs. In essence, a Tombstone Opening is an end of a mourning period where a newly erected Tombstone is unveiled (Beckett, 1990). The Tombstone unveiling is the central aspect of the entire ceremony and event; however, other aspects are also involved in this event such as a feast, singing, dancing, speeches and more (Singe, 1979). The event typically happens a year to 2 years or more after the person dies, or when the family of the deceased can afford to arrange the ceremony. The Tombstone Opening is typically a very significant event in the life of a person whether it is for a family member or friend and brings family from different islands and the Australian mainland to the event (Smith & Bird, 2000).

In Tombstone Openings, many people have responsibilities and duties that they need to fulfil to help and ensure the event runs well. There is a head person, sometimes called a Mariget, who is assigned to organise and direct the Tombstone Opening ceremony (Australian Screen, 2000). This head person is nominated by the family and could be a close family member or friend to the deceased and could be male or female, but it is often an in-law of the deceased. In Torres Strait society, in-laws normally have considerable responsibility and say in cultural matters. Nonetheless, the head person typically allocates duties to different family members or friends in the organisation of the event. Some duties tend to be gender specific (e.g. hunting for dugong or turtle meat) while other duties tend not to be. Thus, there are various duties before, during and after the Tombstone Opening that need to be performed and fulfilled by the family and community.

For the in-game implementation of the lead up to the Tombstone Opening, the player has duties allocated to fulfil. The player's responsibility are to collect Warups (drums), mats, Waps (spears), turtle and dugong for the ceremony and feast on Waiben. The different duties of the player served as story progression and objectives in the game. In different sections of the game, we placed campfires to signal checkpoints. However, the campfires also indicated progression in the gameplay and significant storyline events such as a meeting and trading with Papua New Guinea traders which is a common real-life practice (Boigu Island Community Council 1991, 1991; CairnsILS, 2009). See Figure 4.1 for a screenshot of a campfire location. Torres Strait culture and its associated protocols are represented in the very basis of the game because your purpose in the game is to fulfil your cultural responsibilities that will culminate in the Tombstone Opening at the end of the game.

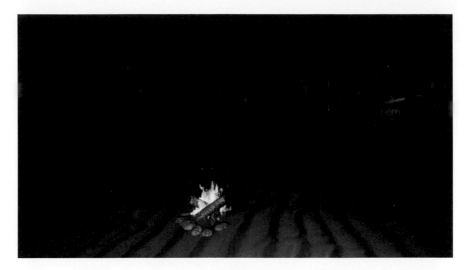

Figure 4.1 Player sitting around a campfire on Mabuyag. Mabuyag is the first checkpoint where you start your journey to gather items for the Tombstone Opening. The campfire signals different points in the story and meeting different people through your journey [in-game screenshot].

Torres Strait item – the Warup

The Warup is a Torres Strait drum used in many musical compositions and is often played at dances, ceremonies, or other performances. The Warups come in different shapes and sizes, but are typically long and narrow. The Warup is traditionally made with wood from the Torres Straits or Papua New Guinea with snakeskin/goanna skin used for the batter head (top of the Warup). Beeswax droplets can be applied to the batter head to create different sounds each drum. Because of the Warup's common use and place in music accompanying dances, ceremonies and events, the Warup has a special significance for many Torres Strait Islanders. See Figure 4.2 for a photo of Warups.

The Tombstone Opening has become deeply embedded in Torres Strait culture and before, during and after the event, there are cultural protocols and duties that need to be fulfilled. TSVR was designed to replicate the lead up to the Tombstone Opening and the narrative and premise of the game is representative of the duties that needed to be fulfilled for the event. Through embedding the Tombstone Opening event as the premise of the game, we were respectfully using relational knowledges and practices that are known universally among the Torres Strait community and

Figure 4.2 Two different-sized Warups [photograph].

encoding them into the gaming structure of TSVR (Brayboy et al., 2012). Through the gameplay, players are required to respect the cultural protocols and carry out their responsibility as a part of the community (Brayboy et al., 2012). Here, cultural protocols and duties are embodied in the very premise of the game and it is your duty as the player to follow the protocols and fulfil these cultural duties as a part of the community. In addition to the premise of the game, the project team tried to represent culture in different ways throughout landscape, seascape and sky in-game.

Connection to land, ocean and culture in design

In Torres Strait culture, there is a deep connection to Place with many of the stories relating to the islands surrounding ocean and sky. For some communities, culture can come from the interaction between the people, environment and arising experiences between these elements. For some Torres Strait Islanders, stories can be created from their understanding and experiences of the environment. Similar understandings exist for a variety of other cultures such as in some communities in India where mountains, the landscape, water and geography of the country are seen as culturally significant and religiously sacred and are tied into various cultural and religious stories and practices (Bhardwaj, 1983; Eck, 2012; Singh, 2020). Cultural stories and metaphysical understanding of the local communities are attached to the landscape itself. From this perspective, the culture and related practices can be strongly shaped by both the experiences of a people and the physical geography where these people live and consider their home.

There are also similar understandings in the Torres Straits. For example, there are stories in the Torres Straits such as the story of Gelam who rode a Dugong across the Torres Straits from Moa to Mer and he stopped at various islands along the way (Gela, 1993; statelibraryqld, 2011a). Prior to leaving Moa, Gelam packed fruits, vegetables and other plants for the journey and during his travels Gelam left some of these plants on each of the islands he visited. Before Gelam left, his mother walked out into the ocean begging him not to leave. In today's setting, if you were to travel to Mer you can see a hill in the shape of a dugong and if you stayed on the islands Gelam visited you can find similar fruit, vegetables and plants. You can also find a protruding rock outside of Moa which is said to be Gelam's mother. Here, both the landscape and environment are intimately intertwined with the cultural stories and metaphysical understandings of the Torres Straits.

In TSVR, we tied some of these elements of the island stories and geography together. For example, in Torres Strait stories from Dauan, Giz is a Dogai who lives on Dauan and sits on a stone lookout (Lawrie, 1970). In the traditional stories, Giz also shape shifts into an octopus to ambush an unsuspecting victim. In TSVR, if you are exploring Dauan and encounter her, you will see an octopus integrated into her game model which relates back to the original story. See Figure 4.3 for an in-game screenshot of Giz. If you travel to Dauan in-game, you will find there are an abundance of rocks and boulders on the island. Similarly, if you were to travel to Dauan in person, the island has many boulders and rock formations. Here, the physical geography and landscape is tied into traditional stories which is then reflected in TSVR.

Unintentionally, the game world was divided into three levels: the land, the sea and the sky. Each of these levels had elements that contained and depicted cultural elements to the player. The land is important because it is where the people live. The ocean is important as a considerable variety of food comes from the sea with many Torres Strait totems also being associated with the sea. The sky is important in Torres Strait culture as the star constellations in the sky relate to stories, and tend to have practical uses for understanding the seasons and for navigating the islands.

Figure 4.3 In TSVR, Giz can be found in a rock cave on Dauan. Her in-game asset was modelled around her story where she turns into an octopus. The in-game representation shows an octopus, a shell and seaweed integrated into her model [in-game screenshot].

Thus through the level design of TSVR, we are exercising respect towards community and relational knowledges which guided what the project team embedded into TSVR (Brayboy et al., 2012). So, wherever the player was traveling and viewing, there were elements of culture reflected in their sight. In addition to the visual depictions, culture was communicated through the audio narration by the Torres Strait Elder.

Narration and story characters

Walking through the game, the Elder guides and speaks to the player throughout the journey in-game. The Elder explains the storyline of the lead up to the Tombstone Opening and your responsibility in the lead up to the event. The Elder also advises you how to navigate and interact with the game world. Not only does he talk you through the importance of the Tombstone Opening and your duties, he also imparts knowledge about the Torres Straits such as the seasons, animal life cycles and story characters you will encounter in-game. This approach within the game matches the learning method of listening and then doing.

The Elder was also pivotal in developing and deciding the Torres Strait story characters to insert into the game. While the main storyline of the game was the preparation for the Tombstone Opening, the team decided players should be able to encounter other cultural elements through exploring and moving around the different islands. For example, we added story characters that further built on the cultural premise of the game and communicated the stories of the islands.

For example, a Dogai story character reflected in-game was Metakurab (Lawrie, 1970). Metakurab's story originates from Boigu and in her story, she sleeps in a guinea fowl nest until disturbed by men searching for food. In the story, Metakurab

Figure 4.4 Dogai Metakurab next to a large guinea fowl mound where she sleeps and hides. Her home area is abundant with butterflies which she commands [in-game screenshot].

controls insects, but quite noticeably, butterflies form a part of these swarms. You know that Metakurab is close when butterflies begin to appear and then gradual swarms arrive. She would weaponise these insects against villages on the islands. In-game, you will also find her on Boigu if you explore the island as there is an over-grown path to the guinea fowl nest where she lives. As you follow the path, you will gradually see more butterflies until there are swarms of butterflies around a guinea fowl nest. Behind the nest, the player will find Metakurab who is adorned in grasses from the area which the guinea fowl use in their nests. This in-game representation is another example of the physical environment and traditional story being tied to the game depiction. Creative license was taken to depict the Dogais in new ways, as representations in other media depict the Dogais as having large ears. Nonetheless, where possible, efforts were still made to tie the in-game depictions back to the original stories and environment. See Figure 4.4 for an in-game screenshot of Metakurab.

Other story characters included in the game are Wawa the giant who commands birds (Lawrie, 1970; statelibraryqld, 2011b). In-game as you approach the island where Wawa is located, you will see birds circling over his island. Another character is Kupas who is a benevolent character and hunts the Dogai (Gela, 1993). On Buru (Turnagain Island) you will find Kupas who has defeated several Dogais. Again, efforts have been made to tie the story characters back to their original stories and depict them this way in-game. See Figures 4.5 and 4.6 for in-game screenshots of Wawa and Kupas, respectively.

These in-game characters were not represented in an exact retelling of the past stories. Instead, the game featured these characters to give insight into the variety of stories within the Torres Straits and how those stories were often tied to the islands and sometimes specific places. These stories were relational and respect was

Figure 4.5 Wawa the giant stands over a giant pyre and flocks of birds circle around his island. In TSVR, he stays on an isolated island with his bird helpers [in-game screenshot].

paid to their original story, albeit reinterpreted by the Elder and myself to fit into TSVR (Brayboy et al., 2012). In this way, we were also assuming a responsibility to the community and were considering how to respectfully integrate the original stories into the game. However, one aspect which was not depicted was the Torres Strait people and this game design decision was not made lightly.

Figure 4.6 In past stories, Kupas attacks Dogai, but is sometimes depicted as a small crab. In TSVR, he is seen next to defeated Dogais; however, I have depicted him as giant crab [in-game screenshot].

Depiction of Torres Strait Islander people and cultural artefacts

While building the island world of TSVR, the decision was made not to depict Torres Strait Islander people in-game. Given the size of the team, resources and time available, the team found it difficult to create lifelike models of Torres Strait people that would match the look and feel of the game. Although representing Torres Strait people is an important aspect of reflecting the community, the Elder and I decided inaccurate depictions would have been far less genuine and respectful. Unfortunately, we were also not able to source any appropriate models from any 3D model and assets stores. The only human models that were available included different cultures and communities from Europe, Asia and Africa, but not Indigenous Australian models, let alone Torres Strait Islander models more specifically.

This issue also highlights a bias not only within games, but also in the options available to build game worlds. With limited resources and time, our project team had to rely on assets and models from online 3D models and asset stores to build the world. These online shops while maintaining a large collection are still limited in some of the selections they sell. For example, if you were building a world set in a medieval English countryside, there are more options to source assets and 3D models than building a world set in the Torres Straits. Assets can provide further in-depth cultural detail and flavour to the game world, yet a lack of asset availability can limit the world building for certain cultures and communities.

The limitations of available assets online can also be seen as a limitation of the ways the story can be told. A designer friend said that these assets and 3D models are like words which you use to tell your story and culture through the game world. In this way, we have less words and ways to describe our story in its full richness and cultural depth, compared to other cultures which may have access to more assets from online stores. In TSVR, we had to offset this lack of assets with other ways to communicate culture, such as through sketches and narration from the Elder as well as a small selection of in-house modelled Torres Strait assets. The simpler assets that we were able to create from scratch were the Tombstone, the grave coping and Torres Strait islander artefacts.

A key aspect to the Tombstone Opening is the unveiling ceremony where the cloth covering the headstone and the coping is removed. Depending on the family there could be different objects under the cloth. These objects can range from money that could be pinned in the wrapping to artefacts and objects such as mats, warups (drums), waps (harpoon) and spears. The Tombstone and cultural objects were imagined in the original sketches for the game and created as assets for the game. See Figure 4.7 for the Elder's sketches of a Tombstone at the Tombstone Opening event. Also see Figure 4.8 for a representation of a Tombstone and coping with accompanying Torres Strait artefacts and other items.

The Elder also helped guide one of the undergraduate student designers through the 3D modelling process of cultural objects that were used in TSVR. These modelled objects included the design of a Warup (Torres Strait Drum), a mat, the tombstone and coping, a spear and a Wap (harpoon). The Warup, spear

Figure 4.7 The Tombstone, gravesite coping, shells and Torres Strait artefacts. This sketch appears at the end game to signify the Tombstone Opening and the unveiling of the Tombstone [sketch]. Sketch by Gehamat Loban.

Figure 4.8 At the beginning of the game, players will encounter a Tombstone site with Torres Strait artefacts, food and flowers on the grave. This Tombstone gravesite provides a stylised example of a traditional arrangement at a Tombstone Opening [in-game screenshot].

and Wap required close guidance because they are objects that are quite specific to the Torres Strait in aesthetic design and use. I provided pictures of the Wap, spear and Warup to the undergraduate student designer to follow. However, he was still closely guided by the Elder who has used the Wap, spear and Warup, and has intimate knowledge about objects workings including the different Wap heads and spearheads. For example, the Kuirir (jagged head) for the Wap and Tata (three-pronged or multi-pronged head) for the spear (Boigu Island Community Council 1991, 1991; Wilson, 1988, 1993). Throughout this process, respect for the Elder's perspective and the relational knowledge he maintains was paramount as well as respect for the community which shaped design decisions around the inclusion and exclusion of different game assets and cultural depictions (Brayboy et al., 2012). The Elder also sketched cultural story characters that were used in the game.

Sketches and constellations

The Elder significantly contributed to the game through sketches of various story characters and animals. Initially, these sketches were a valuable part of the brain-storming process and helped determine the cultural elements included in the game. Other sketches were used during the end game and credits. However, more impor-tantly, some of the sketches became 3D assets used in the game to depict constel-lations in the sky. Constellations play an important part in Torres Strait knowledge and stories which are linked to seasonal calendars and have a navigational use (Sharp, 1993). Moreover, the stars and constellations are often intimately linked to the stories and characters of the Torres Straits. For example, Taigai, who is depicted in-game, is a Zugubal who has control over the wind and comes from the stars. In his story, he banishes his crew as punishment for stealing. So when you look up at the stars, Tagai is depicted in the south, while his crew are opposite to him in the north of the sky (Hamacher, 2013; Lawrie, 1970; Mura Gubal Gedira, 2007). In TSVR, Tagai was depicted as an abstracted constellation. Also depicted in the sky are abstracted versions of the Kaygas (shovel nose shark), the pelican, Baidam (the shark), githalai (crab) and a Dogai. See Figure 4.9 for a sketch of githalai and Figure 4.10 for a sketch of the pelican.

The depicted constellations were not exact replicas of how the constellations appear in the sky, but rather abstracted versions which were essentially projecting and illuminating the 3D sketch assets in the night sky. The intent here was not to provide exact and hyper-realistic depictions of the constellations and astronomy as it is in real life. Instead, these constellations were used to indicate the stories associated with the knowledge of the sky and then how these were used in practi-cal ways to live and navigate the environment. We felt this approach was more impactful with the aims of the game than more exact depictions of the stars. How-ever, the general locations of the constellations in-game were correct. For exam-ple, Tagai was placed in the south of the sky where it is said his spear forms the southern cross (Art Gallery of NSW, 2021; Sharp, 1993). The depiction of Tagai drawn by the Elder was not mapped to the exact constellations of stars, but the

Figure 4.9 The githalai appears in-game and is based on the Watharrau Githalai (Mura Gubal Gedira, 2007) [sketch]. Sketch by Gehamat Loban.

Figure 4.10 The pelican that also appears as a constellation in-game. This in-game constellation shifts according to the seasons and in-game progress (Noordhuis-Fairfax, 2007) [sketch]. Sketch by Gehamat Loban.

Figure 4.11 Original sketch of Tagai before conversion into a 3D asset to be used in-game. Tagai is an important and universal story figure and known across the Torres Straits (Lawrie, 1970; Sharp, 1993) [sketch]. Sketch by Gehamat Loban.

intent was not an exact representation. Rather the Elder had his own stylistic approach the Elder wanted to depict in-game. See Figures 4.11 and 4.12 for a sketch of Tagai and the in-game screenshot of the Tagai constellation. See Figures 4.13 and 4.14 for a sketch of Baidam the Shark and the in-game screenshot of the Baidam constellation.

Figure 4.12 An abstracted version of the Tagai constellation in the night sky. Tagai can be seen in the south holding his spear [in-game screenshot].

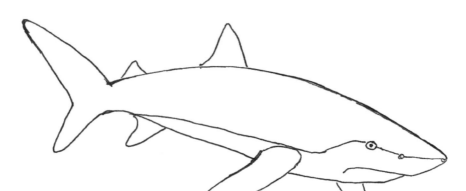

Figure 4.13 The original sketch of Baidam by the Elder before being converted into a 3D model in TSVR. Baidam can be seen in the north of the sky (Haddon et al., 1912; Hamacher, 2015; Hamacher et al., 2016) [sketch]. Sketch by Gehamat Loban.

Figure 4.14 Baidam the shark is in the north of the sky and hangs above Boigu where you first travel to inside the game. Islands are less visible at night, but Baidam can serve as a tool to navigate [in-game screenshot].

Torres Strait story – Tagai

Tagai, like Gelam, is a cultural figure that is known universally among all Torres Strait Islanders. He is a Zugubal which is a superhuman that can control lighting, thunder, rain and wind. Zugubals can also control the temper of the seas. In TSVR, Tagai features as a constellation in the south of the sky holding the southern cross as his spear.

In TSVR, constellations appear every night and can be used as a method to navigate without the vision typically provided during the day. As you progress through the game, one of the constellations would change position and angle to signify a change in the season which was also indicated by the narrator as well. While the constellations were not exact or hyper-realistic depictions, the general locations of the constellations in the sky were correct and conveyed the abstracted Torres Strait knowledge of the sky and constellations. The sketches produced by the Elder took centre stage in TSVR and he shared his own interpretation of community knowledge though the game. At the same time, the Elder was still respectful and responsible to the community and their understandings of the constellations as he conducted his own research to gain new perspectives that were also integrated into the game (Brayboy et al., 2012). These constellation positions were aligned with the geography and layout of the islands in-game.

Islands depicted in-game

The abstracted design of the Island world was strongly shaped by the Elder's and my own cultural connections and lineage to different islands. So, the significant Torres Strait Islands that were included in TSVR were mostly around the Western, Top-Western and Inner Island groups which included Mabuyag, Boigu, Dauan, Saibai and Waiben. Another island, Buru, was also included but there is no community on this island. Although the game could have included the Island groups of Central and Eastern Islands, we felt that we could not speak with any great authority or do any real justice to the islands in any great detail. An abstracted partial map of the Torres Straits was also crafted specifically to help the player navigate the game world. See Figure 4.15 for a screenshot of the in-game map. Therefore, the focus remained on a selection of islands in the Western, Top-Western and Inner Island groups of the Torres Strait.

While the stylistic depiction of the islands in-game was quasi-realistic, the decision was made to abstract the geography of the islands and of the area. Therefore the layout in-game is an abstracted version of the real-life layout of the islands and waters (Torres Strait Regional Authority, 2020). In-game the islands are closer and viewable from other islands to allow the player to see where they can travel, which is not the case in real life. In-game, the islands are geographically smaller, so the players do not get lost, but the player is still able to explore different sections and the layout of the islands. Smaller abandoned islands were enlarged to place story characters on them. Again, representations were used based on what we could

Figure 4.15 The Torres Strait Virtual Reality map focused on islands and Island groups where the project lead and Elder had strong connection and experience, especially Mabuyag and Boigu [in-game screenshot].

realistically create and the assets that were available from online asset stores. See Figure 4.16 for a screenshot of a view from Mabuyag.

Various animals and plants are also depicted in-game and vary from island to island. Many of these animals and plants aligned with real-life locations and habitats (Beckett, 1990; Gaffney, 1989; Leonard et al., 1995). There are manta rays, turtles, dugong, various fish, coral reefs, deer, boar, crayfish, squid, crocodile, palm trees and a Malay Apple tree. In some cases, we tried to link these animals or plants to

Figure 4.16 Sunrise on Mabuyag in the Torres Straits with a close view to Buru and a distant view of Boigu. Buru and Boigu would not be viewable at the same time in real life as depicted here, but the islands were abstracted to make navigation in-game easier [in-game screenshot].

Figure 4.17 Spotting a stingray at Kai Reef during the day. The reef is also home to a variety of other marine life including corals, various fish and sharks [in-game screenshot].

various parts of the Torres Straits where you would typically find them. For example, we placed deer on Saibai as the Elder had observed deer swimming over from the Papua New Guinea mainland to Saibai. Turtles can also be found at the surface of the water if they were mating or could be found on land if they were laying eggs. In some places, we placed plants and animals on various islands with specific commentary such as for the Malay Apples. If the Malay Apple tree was in close proximity the narrators would comment on how they are fruiting in the Naigai season (Mura Gubal Gedira, 2007). We believed these aspects communicated a feeling and detail of the Torres Straits in-game. See Figures 4.17–4.26 for screenshots of various animals, plants and habitats from TSVR.

Figure 4.18 Kai reef during the daytime and spotting a dugong which must be collected for the Tombstone Opening [in-game screenshot].

Figure 4.19 An underwater view of the Rainbow Crayfish (Tropical Rock Lobster) march from the Torres Straits to Papua New Guinea as part of their breeding cycle (CSIRO, 1986). In the past, Singe (2003) describes huge numbers of crayfish that formed forests of brown feelers given their abundance [in-game screenshot].

The project team also inserted other environmental features into TSVR such as a shifting tide mechanic. The mechanic was based on real tidal cycles and intended to raise awareness of the tides in the Torres Straits (McCully, 2006). In-game, the mechanic simulated the 4 ebbs and flows throughout a standard day (higher high water, lower low water, lower high water and higher low water).

Figure 4.20 Malay Apples along with mangos and bananas are just some of the fruits that can be found in the Torres Straits. In TSVR, we can see a Malay Apple tree and a boar eating ripened fruit that has dropped off the tree [in-game screenshot].

Figure 4.21 The narrator discusses how the squid are plentiful as they are now in breeding
season. In this screenshot, the player sees a group of squid at nighttime which
is a common time to fish for squid [in-game screenshot].

We had placed sandbanks as obstacles in the game which would surface at certain
times in the day and night. In response, the player would often have to navigate
around the sandbanks. Collectively, TSVR drew from a variety of sources to inform the details of the island world. Information used to design the TSVR game
world was obtained from the lead designers' experiences, the Elder's experiences,

Figure 4.22 A player view of underneath a Manta Ray in the ocean [in-game screenshot].

Figure 4.23 In TSVR, you can find crocodiles and in this screenshot the player has spotted a crocodile at night with a torch. In real life, you can sometimes hear patting and shifting of the sand at night which means crocodiles are near [in-game screenshot].

community input and Torres Strait Islanders knowledge learnt through rigorous research. This breadth of understanding across the Torres Straits indicates how knowledge is relational and shared within the community, and how the community respects, relates and produces knowledge from and about their surroundings (Brayboy et al., 2012).

Figure 4.24 Player encountering a deer in TSVR. In real life, deer have been spotted on Saibai, and also travel between Saibai and the Papua New Guinea mainland. In the Torres Straits, some deer are native while others have been introduced within the last 100 years or so [in-game screenshot].

Figure 4.25 Turtles on the beach on Mabuyag with one turtle crawling towards the player [in-game screenshot].

TSVR implementation and use

We implemented TSVR in four different classes at the University of New South Wales. Initially, we deployed TSVR in a Game Design class to be used as an exemplar for creating a game for learning that used new technology (i.e. VR). Later in an Indigenous Cultural Studies class, we implemented TSVR to show how Indigenous

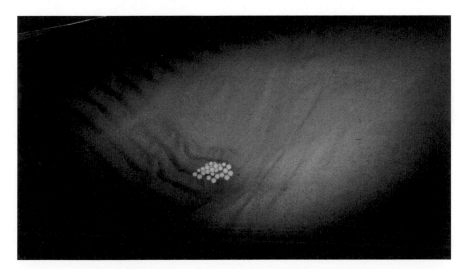

Figure 4.26 Player finding turtle eggs. The Torres Strait is a central location for sea turtles to lay their eggs. After traveling the world's oceans, turtles come back to lay their eggs in the Torres Straits. In the Torres Strait, turtle eggs are a valuable source of food; however, we always ensure never to take more than we need and leave most of the eggs to hatch to allow the cycle to continue [in-game screenshot].

culture is being represented in new mediums. The approach of this class aligned with the Torres Strait cultural palm philosophy of how culture can be represented in new but deep forms that still draw upon existing cultural traditions and practices.

We also implemented TSVR in an Environmental Policy class to show the connection between lived experience and way of life, and Native Title and other policy related to Indigenous culture and communities. For example, in-game you will approach and trade with Papua New Guinea traders who have travelled to nearby islands and are selling items to the communities in the Top-Western Island group of the Torres Straits. If you were to travel to the Torres Straits in real life, there are policies in place to facilitate Torres Strait and PNG traditional activities such as trade between communities. In an Education class focused on Indigenous Issues, we implemented TSVR to show how cultural protocols and processes were applied in the development of the game, i.e. community participation. This community approach will be further discussed in Chapter 5, but the main premise is how we approached community participation and engaged in cultural protocols to construct the game. We also showcased TSVR in summer and winter schools for visiting Indigenous adolescents and other age groups. The intent of the sessions were to encourage Aboriginal and Torres Strait Islander adolescents to consider STEM as a career choice. The showcasing of the game at these school sessions were also opportunities to obtain feedback on the game in both technical/game design and at a cultural level.

Torres Strait art – traditional etchings and lino prints

A common contemporary form of Torres Strait art are lino prints. Lino prints are typically of Torres Strait stories, everyday life, history, the islands and ocean, or other cultural aspects. While lino prints are a more contemporary art form, this art practice finds its origins in traditional etchings and artistic carvings that had long existed in Torres Strait society. The etchings were carved into artistic object such as figures, but they were also engraved into household and everyday objects such as jewellery, wearable apparel, combs, smoking pipes and so on.

It should be noted that we used the game primarily as learning materials with TSVR not available publicly. We made this decision based on consideration of cultural protocols and we also wanted to further refine the game's technical elements as well considerations of the ownership of the game itself. The game development and consultation was finalised, and the game project concluded. TSVR remains restricted for use in university and educational contexts. I believe that TSVR had sufficient community participation for the purposes of learning materials at a university. A playable version is only accessible upon request.

The TSVR heavily involved the community in shaping the project outcome with a highly relational framework influencing the game product (Brayboy et al., 2012).

Reciprocity was central to this process as were relationships with various Torres Strait people involved as well as the broader Indigenous and non-Indigenous community providing input into the project (Brayboy et al., 2012). Reciprocity came in the form of financial compensation for certain community members. However, the project also exercised reciprocity through the design leader spending and volunteering time at several university winter/summer schools and implementing TSVR in various university units as well as showcasing the game at other events. For the Elder, the greatest investment you can make is spending time with another and this approach formed the basis for the reciprocity within TSVR project. Respect and responsibility to the community were upheld with all participants by taking their feedback into consideration which often influenced and shaped the game design. The implementation and use of TSVR with the Indigenous community in Sydney and wider Australia fundamentally shaped the game. The community implementation and feedback was a significant part of the community involvement aspect of the project. The community involvement aspect upheld the notions of relationality, responsibility, respect and reciprocity throughout the process (Brayboy et al., 2012).

Conclusion

In building the TSVR project, we tried to balance cultural depictions in-game with the time, resources and staff that we had. We made many of these design decisions based on the cultural context and considerations of the Torres Straits. Unintentionally, the game development process and design decision aligned with CIRM and its four elements of relationality, responsibility, respect and reciprocity (Brayboy et al., 2012). These four principles are sound approaches for consideration in not only research, but were also applicable in a culturally centred game design process. It should be noted that other projects may vary in their game design approach given their own cultural, technical and creative considerations. In our project I would like to highlight a few specific aspects shaped by cultural practices and considerations:

- The project team represented culture and community within the game wherever it was feasible and achievable within time, resource and staff constraints. In TSVR, the very premise of the game was to collect items for the Tombstone Opening with the player observing and carrying out the cultural obligations and protocols. Throughout the game design process, smaller specific details of cultural knowledge and stories in-game were inserted in a variety of different sections and places to add further cultural depth to the game. Most aspects of the game's narrative and world building were undertaken with culture in mind.
- The level of detail and cultural relevance depicted in-game was important to relate back to the real-life culture, community and place, and provided a level of cultural depth and genuineness. For example, the team carefully depicted the various animals, plants and geographies that were specific to the Torres Straits, or even more specific to each island in some cases. These specific cultural and environmental depictions were often informed by real experiences and confirmed by rigorous research from books, articles and other media. This attention

to detail and specificity improved the cultural representations in the game and helped avoid blanket depictions of community. Consider the different Native American communities who are often portrayed as a hodgepodge of various Native American cultures and stereotypes rather than the specifics of each nation or community (Fahey, 2016; LaPensée, 2008; Longboat, 2019). Typically, the more specificity the better.

• However, our attempt to embed culture in-game, was balanced with the constraints of our resources, time and staff. For example, there were no people represented as it was deemed not appropriate to use another community to represent Torres Strait Islander people. There were no resources, time or staff to create custom models of Torres Strait Islander people. Instead, the culture and community were communicated through other aspects such as the game's premise, the narrator and cultural stories and knowledge depicted in-game. These situations will require design and ethical decisions that game designers will need to reflect on in order to develop the best solutions.

• Community participation and involvement was at the centre of the game design and began at the very foundation of the project. For example, the Elder help shaped the game's premise and contributed assets in the form of the voice lines and sketches, both of which formed key features in the game in the form of the game narrator and constellations illuminated at night. This community centred approach continued throughout the game development in the playtest and QA processes.

Through the design process, the team were not trying to replicate exactly real-life experiences or history. Instead, we were trying to capture the spirit of a cultural practice, and communicate and build around what we could represent of the culture and community in-game. We centred the premise of the game on one aspect of deep culture which was the cultural practice and tradition of mourning someone close who has passed away. We achieved this approach through the representation of the Tombstone Opening, and building the player's journey around this entire premise. The cultural customs, practice and way of life of trading and hunting were also integrated as key checkpoints. The end of the game concludes in attending the ceremony of the Tombstone Opening. At the same time, we tried to depict the geography, animals, plants, constellations and stories of the Torres Straits to provide a strong cultural context to the VR experience. Here, we embedded deep cultural aspects into the game that were reflective of the islands and had real meaning to us. This game is not an exact replica of the real-life process leading up to the Tombstone Opening as parts are abstracted or sections of the process not depicted. However, the game design came from the community and a perspective of deep cultural consideration. For us, the game is a representation of a deep cultural Torres Strait perspective and practice.

In conclusion, the project team had an approach to game design that put culture first and highly valued input from the community to shape the game. Not all games will encounter the same issues as TSVR, however, there are specific considerations and design decisions that designers can implement to more deeply reflect different cultures and communities in-game. Above all, I would say that cultural experiences of the community including the Elder, the wider community and myself along with the backing of rigorous research, strongly guided the project's direction and overall team conduct. Therefore, I recommend to designers a broader three-pronged strategy to integrating cultural representations into video games and the game design process. This three-pronged approach includes community participation, cultural immersion, and rigorous research. I would suggest that by far the most important and direct way to faithfully represent cultures and communities in-game is through community participation. Community participation can occur in a number of ways throughout the project and can range from the leader of the game project being from the community itself to consulting cultural knowledge holders to including people from the culture in the playtest and quality assurance processes.

References

Art Gallery of NSW. (2021*). Gail Mabo – 'Under the stars' for kids.* https://www.youtube.com/watch?v=z5u-VDFAjfA

Australian Screen. (2000). *Tombstone Unveiling – Education notes.* https://aso.gov.au/titles/documentaries/tombstone-unveiling/clip2/

Beckett, J. (1990). *Torres Strait Islanders: Custom and colonialism.* Cambridge University Press.

Bhardwaj, S. M. (1983). *Hindu places of pilgrimage in India: A study in cultural geography* (Vol. 14). University of California Press.

Bogost, I. (2007). *Persuasive games: The expressive power of videogames.* MIT Press.

Boigu Island Community Council 1991 (1991). *Boigu: Our history and culture.* Aboriginal Studies Press.

Brayboy, B. M., Gough, H. R., Leonard, B., Roehl, R., & Solyom, J. A. (2012). Reclaiming scholarship: Critical indigenous research methodologies. In S. D. Lapan, ML. T. Quartoli & F.J. Riemer (Eds.), *Qualitative research: An introduction to methods and designs* (pp. 423–450). Jossey-Bass.

CairnsILS. (2009). *Boigu Island Traders.* https://www.youtube.com/watch?v=FPt41MD72O0

Eck, D. L. (2012). *India: A sacred geography.* Harmony.

Elu, M. (2004). Cooking, walking, and talking cosmology: An Islander woman's perspective of religion. In R. Davis (Ed.), *Woven histories, dancing lives: Torres Strait Islander identity, culture and history* (pp. 140). Aboriginal Studies Press. https://search.informit.org/doi/10.3316/informit.008918914255709

Fahey, M. (2016). *Killer instinct's thunder gets a more culturally accurate outfit.* https://www.kotaku.com.au/2016/12/killer-instincts-thunder-gets-a-more-culturally-accurate-outfit/

Gaffney, E. (1989). *Somebody now: The autobiography of Ellie Gaffney, a woman of Torres Strait.* Aboriginal Studies Press.

Gela, A. A. (1993). *Gelam the man from Moa: A legend of the people of the Torres Strait Islands.* Magabala Books.

Haddon, A. C., Rivers, W. H. R., Seligman, C. G., Myers, C. S., McDougall, W., Ray, S. H., & Wilkin, A. (1912). *Reports of the Cambridge anthropological expedition to Torres Straits: Vol. IV: Arts and crafts.* Cambridge University Press.

Hamacher, D. (2013). *A shark in the stars: astronomy and culture in the Torres Strait.* The Conversation. http://theconversation.com/a-shark-in-the-stars-astronomy-and-culture-in-the-torres-strait-15850

Hamacher, D. (2015). Stories from the sky: Astronomy in indigenous knowledge. *The Australian Humanist* (117), 10–11.

Hamacher, D. W., Tapim, A., Passi, S., & Barsa, J. (2016). "Dancing with the stars" – astronomy and music in the Torres Strait. *arXiv Preprint Arxiv:1605.08507*.

LaPensée, B. A. (2008). Signifying the west: Colonialist design in Age of Empires III: The WarChiefs. *Eludamos. Journal for Computer Game Culture*, *2*(1), 129–144.

Lawrie, M. (1970). *Myths and legends of Torres Strait*. University of Queensland Press.

Leonard, D., Beilin, R., & Moran, M. (1995). Which way kaikai blo umi? Food and nutrition in the Torres Strait. *Australian Journal of Public Health*, *19*(6), 589–595.

Longboat, M. (2019). *Terra Nova: Enacting videogame development through Indigenous-led creation*. Concordia University.

McCully, J. G. (2006). *Beyond the moon: A conversational common sense guide to understanding the tides*. World Scientific.

Mura Gubal Gedira. (2007). *Torres Strait Islander – Zugubal*. https://www.qcaa.qld.edu.au/about/k-12-policies/aboriginal-torres-strait-islander-perspectives/resources/seasons-stars

Noordhuis-Fairfax, S. (2007). *The story of Australian printmaking 1801–2005*. https://nga.gov.au/exhibitions/the-story-of-australian-printmaking-1801-2005/#About

Sharp, N. (1993). *Stars of Tagai: The Torres Strait Islanders*. Aboriginal Studies Press.

Singe, J. (1979). *The Torres Strait: People and history*. University of Queensland Press.

Singe, J. (2003). *My island home: A Torres Strait memoir*. University of Queensland Press.

Singh, R. P. (2020). Sacrality and waterfront sacred places in India: Myths and the making of place. In *Sacred Waters* (pp. 80–94). Routledge.

Smith, E. A., & Bird, R. L. B. (2000). Turtle hunting and tombstone opening: Public generosity as costly signaling. *Evolution and Human Behavior*, *21*(4), 245–261.

statelibraryqld. (2011a). *The story of Atmer and Gelam told by Elimo Tapim*. https://www.youtube.com/watch?v=nYcx8ios9cU&list=PLrqonDHggzO8SddkIQRqxdRWJlpv90y7p&index=6

statelibraryqld. (2011b). *The story of Wawa told by Walter Waria*. https://www.youtube.com/watch?v=Pr_RmXLG-js

Torres Strait Regional Authority. (2020). *Regional map*. http://www.tsra.gov.au/the-torres-strait/regional-map

Wilson, L. (1988). *Thathilgaw Emeret Lu: A handbook of traditional Torres Strait Islands material culture*. Department of Education.

Wilson, L. (1993). *Kerkar Lu: Contemporary arterfacts of the Torres Strait Islanders*. Department of Education.

5   Community participation in game design

This chapter discusses the importance of community participation in the design and development of games, in particular TSVR. This community-based design approach is the most direct and inclusive way to embed deep understandings of culture in-game. However, while community participation is the most direct method, there are different approaches to embedding community into a game development project. Community involvement could include having a community member as a part of the game design team, involving the community in the quality assurance (QA) and playset process, embedding a cultural knowledge holder into the project, working with professional cultural experts, holding a game jam or any combination of these approaches. There are also other aspects of community participation to consider such as the structure of the organisation you might approach to participate in the design process as well as related kinship groups.

As a general rule, the earlier the community participates in the project the better. Introducing community involvement in the early stages of the project helps avoid issues that may be raised around the core design and gameplay. These issues may only be realised at a later stage if community participation is introduced after the project is underway. Moreover, introducing community participation earlier also means community members can raise interesting ideas and viewpoints about the culture that the designers may not have considered. These ideas and viewpoints are not always written about or publicly well-known and can only come from lifelong experiences with the culture.

A prime example would be the Torres Strait Island Tombstone Opening which is not a publicly well-known cultural event. Knowledge of the specific details and processes of the event are even less discernible. If you were to depict a Tombstone Opening in-game and not involve the community early on, there may be problematic interpretations of the event given it is the end of a period of mourning. The protocols around the Tombstone Opening can only be addressed, with any real depth, by those from the community who have been to the events over a lifetime. In this case, early community participation is crucial to the success of a cultural game and community participation is a sound approach in any projects involving cultural representations.

DOI: 10.1201/9781003276289-7

Community participation

Community participation is very important for many cultures regardless of whether the output is an art product, policy outcome, a book or, in this case, a game. While community participation is important for cultures and communities all around the world, involvement is typically essential for Indigenous communities, including in Australia. As many Indigenous communities emphasise community participation as a part of cultural practice. Lucashenko (2015) discusses how some Aboriginal communities maintain democratic practices in their community participation and community-wide decision-making. In many Indigenous communities, these equitable community-wide engagement practices manifest as negotiations and deliberations between those in the community. These processes are evident in the community's everyday interactions and problem-solving, through to large-scale and long-standing community decisions. Similar approaches involving community were also implemented when researchers engaged with First Nations people in Canada. First Nations in Canada also valued equal partnership in regards to matters such as research (Castellano, 2014). These practices and approaches to community are also highly valued by many Torres Strait Islanders (Queensland Department of Aboriginal and Torres Strait Islander Policy and Development, 2000).

Smith (1999) has argued for a community participation and a research model called Kaupapa Māori research. This model advocates placing community needs at front and centre of the research in order to resolve community issues and needs. Smith (2015) views Kaupapa Māori research as research "by Māori, for Māori and with Māori" (p. 47). Greer (2010) had a similar approach with a community in Cape York, Australia where the community drove the research project rather than the researchers themselves. Harding (2015) also recognises and discusses similar problems where the research questions and topics are not always set by the communities themselves but rather decided by interest groups outside the communities who fund the research and can influence research agendas and questions. From these perspectives, there is a fundamental shift in the way community participation and research are approached and conducted, and who sets the research agenda and decides what the research questions are.

Historically and even today, research is not well regarded by many Indigenous communities. Some communities have been exposed to poor research standards and studied in highly insensitive ways (Brayboy et al., 2012). As previously discussed, CIRM reverses this approach and instead provides a sound framework where community is centred and drives the research project, and where research can become a method to solve community-identified issues. We can see that CIRM very specifically centres its approach and sub-elements (relationality, responsibility, respect and reciprocity) around community and relationships. Although TSVR was not specifically a research-based project, the practices of community participation provided an excellent foundation for the project that involved Indigenous people. Each of Brayboy et al.'s elements facilitate and support engagement with Indigenous communities. While Brayboy et al. and other authors' methodologies relate to research, the crux of these methodologies is about heavily placing community at the centre of the process and approach of the project.

In the TSVR project, we implemented a similar cultural and community-centred focus from the start of the game development and took steps to involve the Torres Strait and broader Indigenous Australian community. The TSVR project employed several community participation approaches; however, there are various approaches to community participation that can be implemented in a project. One might implement community participation in the project by including:

- A game design leader or team member from the community.
- General community feedback in process as a part of playtesting or QA process.
- Involvement of an Elder or cultural knowledge holder as a consultant or embedding them in the team.
- Involvement of professional experts from the community as a part of the game design process.
- A game jam involving the community.
- Any combination of these approaches to different degrees or other approaches involving community participation.

See Figure 5.1 for the different stages where community might typically be involved in the game development cycle. The more stages the community is involved in typically the better.

COMMUNITY PARTICIPATION IN THE GAME DEVELOPMENT CYCLE

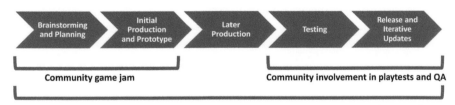

Figure 5.1 This cycle shows approximations of where different community involvement could occur during a game development project. Community game jams might occur in the brainstorming and planning, and initial prototypes stages. Community can also provide effective cultural input in the testing and final phase in the playtesting and QA process. Team members, cultural knowledge holders and professional cultural experts can be involved at any time or throughout the entire length of the game design and development. The more stages the community can be involved in the better [graphical diagram].

The TSVR project integrated community participation into the process by having a community member as the design lead, embedding a knowledge holder into the project team and involving community in the QA and playtest process. Myself as a Torres Strait Islander led the game development project, a Torres Strait Elder was guiding the project and the game design process involved Torres Strait Islander people as well as the wider Indigenous and non-Indigenous community as a part of the playtests and QA. Although each of the listed approaches are valid, some approaches will be more conducive to some projects than others (e.g. some projects might require specialist cultural knowledge or skills). A combination of some or all of these approaches to community participation can also be used to help capture a wider perspective from the community. A combination approach can also support the triangulation of different perspectives as well as promote cultural depth within the project.

Member of community embedded in the game project team

A direct way of involving community and embedding a cultural perspective into a project is to have a member of the community on the team and involved in the game design process. This approach can ensure that in the early development of the game, a person from that culture is involved in the design process and can strongly influence how their community is depicted in-game. LaPensée (2020) in her Indigenous-centred game design draws upon an Anishinaabe-centred methodology called Biskaabiiyang. Biskaabiiyang emphasises connecting with collaborators, making connection through the development cycle and continuing this reconnecting through the process, in addition to being responsible for maintaining the game and its representations as best as possible. LaPensée (2020) also emphasises the Sovereignty, Positionality, Equity, Advocacy, and Reciprocity or the SPEAR framework for the design and development of Indigenous cultural games. The SPEAR framework places a significant emphasis on involving Indigenous people from the very beginning of the process as opposed to just specific inclusions or ticking-the-box approaches to inclusions. Games like *Honour Water* (Pinnguaq, 2016), *Thunderbird Strike* (LaPensée, 2017), and *When Rivers were Trails* (The Indian Land Tenure Foundation, 2019) are examples where the game was led and strongly shaped by LaPensée, as a member of her community, but others in the community members also influenced and shaped the game. Overall, LaPensée et al. (2022) emphasises leading roles for Indigenous community members in the design process from the ground up.

For other communities, such as those in the Indian (South Asian) game industry, some developers are seizing the opportunity to communicate their cultures through integrating more of the region's cultural heritage into their games (Zeiler & Mukherjee, 2022). Zeiler and Mukherjee (2022) discuss how some local game projects are heavily drawing on influences from Hindu stories and other cultural aspects including history, art, music, dance, dress styles and architecture to inform their games. Zeiler and Mukherjee (2022) cite *Raji: An Ancient Epic* (Nodding

Heads Games, 2020) and, a yet-to-be released game, *Antariksha Sanchar* (Antariksha Sanchar, 2022) as games where Indian developers are strongly embedding cultural aspects of the region into their games. Regardless of the approach by the design team, by embedding the community from the very beginning of development, we can help bring a more culturally centred focus to the entire game design and communicate culture depth from the community.

In the TSVR project, as a Torres Strait Islander, I have my own cultural experience and cultural knowledge which I was able to bring to the project from the very beginning. In TSVR, I had the position and responsibility of project leader and game designer, and I ultimately determined and implemented the direction of the game. I also made the final decisions on many of the significant game design choices. In TSVR, any decision around cultural depictions in-game were made in accordance with my family's knowledge and my own understandings of the culture. The cultural depictions in-game were not only a reflection of my own culture and community, but also of how I saw myself and my family. Therefore, I was always careful to ensure I was depicting culture in-game in a way that is respectful and truthful to my community and myself. Being a lead on the project meant I could communicate my own understanding of Torres Strait culture in a genuine way from my own experiences. For me, culture was front, and centre of the game and I believed I was in a position to communicate this directly as the project lead and lead game designer. From the central story line of a Tombstone Opening to the smaller details about the game geography, this project was a vehicle to communicate my understanding of Torres Strait culture.

Collectively, embedding a member of the community being depicted in the game as a lead or member in the game design team seems to be one of the more direct ways to integrate cultural understandings and perspectives into your project. These project leaders or community members can bring their own cultural standpoint to integrate into the project from the very beginning of the game design process and offer perspectives different from someone from outside the culture. The presence of the community member means that their perspective is present throughout the project lifespan. In another approach to community participation, designers can involve community members in the playtest and QA processes of the game development to further embed community perspectives into the game.

Community as a part of playtesting and quality assurance

TSVR deployed a community-based player-centred design to the game development (Sykes & Federoff, 2006). In player-centred design, a significant and important part of the game design process involves engagement with players who play the game or prototype and provide feedback (Salen et al., 2004). Developers then act on this player input to redesign or fine-tune the game. After the initial playtest by players and redesign by the game designers, an iterative process begins to take place where player and developers go back and forth to redesign and fine tune the game. The players are important stakeholders and their views and enjoyment are important in shaping the game. This player-centred iterative process not only helps provide player feedback to shape the product but also provides QA measures to ensure technical issues are resolved and that the overall project is on track to complete its objectives (Feldman, 2005). This process can help designers reasonably ascertain how players enjoy and engage with the game and the kinds of issues that might be encountered in public circulations of the game. The player-centred outcome should ultimately produce a product that has been through heavy player input and guided by player feedback for whom the product is intended.

This process of player-centred design can align with the community participation process. Here, players are members from the community who are necessary in the development of a cultural product or outcome. In the case of TSVR, these two processes of game design/technical refinement and community participation align and work in synchronisation. One component is used to help resolve concerns related to game design and technical issues that are typically resolved through a general player-centred design and rigorous playtests. The other component is used to resolve matters related to cultural protocols and community representation in-game. For example, one piece of feedback received for TSVR was to include more of the local animals. This input served as a means to both improve the game as a whole and fulfil cultural depictions. The addition of more local animals would, from a game design perspective, add further genuine cultural flavour and player engagement with the island world. However, at a cultural level, many local animals serve as totems for different communities, and adding these animals was a further reflection of the cultural and community representation in-game.

> **Torres Strait story – Wawa**
>
> Wawa is a giant being and his story comes from the Western Island group in the Torres Strait, especially Badu Island. He is the main antagonist in the stories and is able to commands birds that carry out his bidding and the harassment of villages. In TSVR, he can be found on an isolated island. As you approach the island, you will notice his birds circle the island signalling his presence.

Aside from myself as the lead developer and the Elder, who will be discussed in the next section, the project team also involved the wider community in TSVR playtests and quality assurance. Several Torres Strait Islander community members played the game and provided their own feedback and experiences in relation to the game. This feedback was compared and contrasted with the teams understanding and experiences and fed into the game design. Comments were collected from four university classes, a number of which had an Indigenous focused content and/ or a group of Indigenous students. I also worked with different sections of the university to showcase a prototype to Indigenous youths during multiple summer schools, winter schools and STEM-related student events at the university and in the community. We discussed and asked them for their thoughts to ascertain their opinions after their gameplay. Some community participation discussions had more impact on the cultural design decisions than other discussions which instead helped refine the technical aspects of the game. In either case, it was important that the process took place with respect to cultural protocols of the community. Overall, the community participation in the playtest and QA phase helped improve the game both from a cultural, and design and technical perspective. Another crucial part of the community participation was the Torres Strait Elder embedded into the team who heavily influenced the project direction and game design.

Elders and cultural knowledge holders

The TSVR project relied heavily on and sought out the guidance of the Torres Strait Elder embedded in the project team. The Elder was a source of deep cultural knowledge as well as being a crucial project contributor. No other community members involved in the project had such in-depth knowledge. These knowledgeable and respected community members may differ from community to community. These community members could be Elders within the community, fluent language speakers, knowledge carriers, or individuals who have deep and intimate lived personal experiences of the culture and connection to the place and community (LaPensée et al., 2022). Similar community participation approaches can be seen in the game design of LaPensée (2014) who developed the game *Survivance* (LaPensée, 2011). *Survivance* was a social impact game that focused on the creation of art to aid the healing which was inflicted on the community from the invasion and colonisation of Turtle Island. In the Survivance project, the project drew heavily upon an Indigenous Elder to inform the game design (LaPensée, 2011). These approaches to community go beyond just cultural inclusion (Parkinson & Jones, 2019) and instead these approaches make the deep and respected knowledge holders of the culture an important part of the game development team. Such knowledge and perspectives are not always reflected in highly digital spaces.

The familial Elder embedded in the TSVR team was involved in making central decisions about the game's storyline and important cultural depictions in-game. He held valuable cultural knowledge from attending and being a part of many Tombstone Openings including for close family, and he knew the Tombstone Opening process intimately. He provided valuable knowledge of the cultural protocols and helped translate them into the design of the game and the storyline of the TSVR where the player has to carry out duties and protocols in the lead up to a Tombstone Opening in-game. His intimate knowledge helped provide specific details about the duties, protocols and different aspects typical to a Tombstone Opening, for example, the items laid on the gravestone bed.

The Elder, prior to the project, was a former primary school teacher for many years and knew how to speak to an audience and helped facilitate learning from the game narrative. Thus, the Elder also fulfilled the role as the narrator for TSVR. As the narrator, the Elder guided the player through the game and towards the completion of each of the objectives as well as introducing the player to differ-ent encounters in-game (e.g. new story characters, natural phenomena, the islands themselves). The Elder's lived experience of the islands meant he could also con-tribute and say with certainty the kinds of animals, plants and geography of each of the islands. This knowledge, in addition to my own experiences and research, meant there could be a more truthful representation of each of the islands depicted in-game. In this way, by serving as the narrator, the Elder could directly guide the player through the world as he saw it and communicate his understandings of the island world with real experience and truth.

The Elder developed and contributed art assets to the project which were used directly in the game. He sketched many depictions to illustrate aspects of the cul-ture and share his knowledge. The project team used these sketches in various ways throughout the game. Some sketches were used as inspiration for creating in-game models, others were used to appear in cinematic shots and credits and in some cases, the sketches were abstracted constellations and were converted into 3D as-sets to then be used as constellations in-game. These constellations were culturally important, serving as a navigational tool in-game (and in real life), but also to tell stories and indicate changes in the environment. The Elder guided the design of the in-game cultural items related to the Tombstone Opening such as the Warup, a mat, a tombstone, a spear and a Wap. Along with the Elder's contributions towards the cultural in-game assets and depictions, his knowledge helped provide deep mean-ing to cultural visuals depicted inside the game.

Collectively, Elders and cultural knowledge holders can provide invaluable cul-tural knowledge and guidance within a project. In TSVR, the Elder's intimate cul-tural knowledge, narration and sketches provided real cultural truth and character to the game that would likely not have been achieved otherwise. In some cases, more specific and niche knowledge and skillsets are required to complete the game and do justice to genuine representation of the culture in-game. In these cases, the project may require a specialised cultural professional or experts with specifics skillsets.

Torres Strait item – the Wap (Torres Strait harpoon)

The Wap is a special Torres Strait harpoon used to hunt larger sea creatures. The head of the harpoon is detachable, but is connected to rope which is strung through loops to a floatable harpoon shaft. Different harpoon heads are used for different creatures. So once the head is attached to the intended target, if the target dives deeper, the handle floats to the surface to then be able to draw in the animal. The Wap is typically used on boats or historically from Naths which were wooden platforms erected in shallower waters. The Wap has a special place for some islanders whose professions and way of life were centred around being hunters. See Figure 5.2 for a photograph of a Wap and Figure 5.3 for a sketch of a Nath.

Figure 5.2 My uncle holding a bamboo Wap. Waps are quite long and can be more than 2 to 3 metres in length [photograph].

Figure 5.3 Hunter on a Nath with a Wap [sketch]. Sketch by Gehamat Loban.

Specialised cultural professional or experts

Another approach to engaging the community is through specialised cultural professionals or experts. This approach will likely be required when there is specific knowledge or skills needed for the game to succeed. For example, Mancini (2018) in her examination of *Māori Pā Wars* (Native Games, 2017) found that the developer used a Kaupapa Māori game Development Methodology in his game design approach and undertook consultations to confirm correct representations of Māori knowledge in the game. However, instead of engaging her kaumatua (Elders), she sought the guidance of professionals with specialised skills and knowledge. The developer suggested that a degree of creative licence was needed to strike a balance between communicating traditional Māori knowledge through an interactive digital platform and ensuring the respect of tikanga Māori which is "the set of beliefs associated with Māori practices and procedures established by whakapapa (ancestors) over time" (Mancini, 2018, p. 72). In this way, cultural experts with specific knowledge and skillsets may be better suited or required to complete and guide a project.

This community participation approach involving specialised cultural professionals or experts has been used in another project, which included myself, where Ong et al. (2022) were modding Wuxia-influenced (Chinese martial arts fantasy) music and saber-sword Wushu martial art moves in to the VR game *Beat Saber* (Beat Games, 2018). In short, *Beat Saber* is a game where the player hits directional boxes flying at them while avoiding moving walls. The correct hitting of these boxes is aligned with a piece of music playing in the background. This combination of music and movement creates a rhythmic gaming experience where the player is moving to the music through the gameplay creating a sort of dance. In this case, both music and the flowing series of moves are required for the game level to function.

Given this gameplay, two professional experts from the Chinese community were involved in the project to strongly shape the mod output (Ong et al., 2022). One expert was a Wushu Grand master and the other expert was a Chinese musician who specialised in various Chinese instruments both of whom were based in Sydney, Australia. The Grandmaster was pivotal in determining how the game mod could be suitably used to teach martial arts and the martial arts moves and techniques that would be suitable to embed into the mechanics of the game. The ultimate goal of the mod and the project was to use the mod as a training tool for those learning Chinese Wushu.

The Chinese musician was also essential to the modding project as *Beat Saber* is a game with a core mechanic around music (Ong et al., 2022). She was needed to determine and create an appropriate song for a rhythmic dance game and was responsible for translating the directions and desired marital art moves directed by the Grand Master. The musician was required to consider and create a piece of Chinese music that would be thoughtfully represented in-game and align with the game's requirements. The musician blended traditional instruments and structures of Chinese music with an upbeat dance rhythm which was required for the game.

She was also pivotal to modding the moves into the game and creating the game level. Overall, her contributions were crucial and helped communicate a sense of deep and genuine culture through her music and by mapping the martial arts moves into the game.

In this approach, the project team placed an emphasis on working closely with two professional experts who could specifically contribute to and guide the project. The specific skills and knowledge of the professional experts involved in the project not only supported the development of a culturally sound project, but their expert-specific knowledge was essential to create the mod in the first place. Hence, professionals and experts from the community were crucial to the project and highly conducive to the aims of the project. Another alternative method to community participation is through the practice of game jams which are fast-paced game development events that can prompt the community to ideate and produce their own games in a short space of time.

Game jam involving the community

A potentially suitable method to quickly engage and ideate games centred on culture or that involve a community is through a game development process called a game jam. A game jam can be defined as "an accelerated opportunistic game creation event where a game is created in a relatively short timeframe exploring given design constraint(s) and end results are shared publically" (Kultima, 2015, p. 8). A prominent example of a game jam process being used to engage culture and community is in a research conducted with the Sámi community (Laiti, 2021; Laiti et al., 2020).

Laiti's research (2021) focuses on a game jam event in 2018 and the Sámi community's output at the end of the process. In total, 6 new games were created at this game jam event by combined teams of programmers from different nationalities and adolescents from the Sámi community. In Sámi culture, both traditional games and play traditions can help preserve Sámi heritage (Laiti, 2021). Games have an important role for empowering Sámi communities and support self-determination. Thus, game jamming in a digital space can be seen as a natural extension to this cultural practice of traditional games. Laiti (2021) suggests that these game jams and their outputs were an opportunity to normalise Sáminess within a game-based context, especially digital games.

Sámi stories, teachings and knowledge were critical in the game design process and these cultural aspects were often built into the foundations of the games. For example, one of the games, Gufihtara Eallu, is centred around a traditional Sámi story that includes a cross-generational elf society, the Kufitar (Laiti, 2021). The game's narrative and premise involve the player passing through the elves' land by hurling an iron object over a reindeer herd. Gufihtara Eallu language options include Northern Sámi, Finnish, and English with the game being playable on a VR platform (Laiti, 2021). This game had Sámi traditional stories, traditional knowledges and the Northern Sámi language integrated into its foundation.

Laiti (2021) discusses the digital árran framework which resulted from this research. Digital árran is a Sámi approach that can be used to assist the process of constructing and sharing knowledge through digital environments. Her model has five key aspects including storytelling, contemporary experiences, teachings, language, and sharing and developing. These elements cumulatively support Indigenous empowerment created in and through games, and help communicate aspects of an Indigenous culture to the player. Laiti et al. (2020) believe that game jamming can become a cultural practice in itself for sustaining cultural heritage as well as providing the opportunity to embed Sámi themes and cultures into a playable cultural artefact. This process involved Sámi and non-Sámi people coming together and working to develop games that represent Sáminess and advocate for Sámi perspectives and themes (Laiti et al., 2020). However, during this process there were also opportunities to share expertise and mentor the community in game development to provide them with the opportunity to start their own projects.

Reciprocity and building community capacity

As mentioned, Laiti (2021) indicated that Sámi people were already creating games before their digital form and that these tools are just a new form of cultural expression. Key to this approach is that Sámi culture and Sámi communities are part of the game development process. In the process, Sámi adolescents were also taught programming to integrate Sámi culture and art into the games. Laiti (2021) advocates working with the Sámi people even if the games are not finished. Here, we can engage in productive failures where there are learnings for both those in and outside the culture involved in the game design process (Kapur, 2008). This community engagement is a process of engaging with the community and sharing in the spirit of reciprocity.

Similarly, if you do consider embedding a member of the community in your team in addition to capitalising on cultural expertise, these placements also provide opportunities to develop the skills of those within the community and build their capacity to tell their own stories in the future. It is important to give back to the community, and to build the capacity of the community as some communities do not have the technical expertise, or are just beginning their journey in building their own games (LaPensée et al., 2022). In this way, game design projects are not only intended to output a product at the end of the project while working with the community, but also help to promote skillsets within the community being depicted to let them pursue their own game projects.

Reciprocity with the community can come in many forms and is not only about building up the skillsets of the community. Game designers and creators' contributions in time and resources are also a way of giving back to the community. All contributions are appreciated and work towards building genuine relationships with the community. However, you also need to acknowledge and respect that the community are providing their time and cultural knowledge to you and the project as a part of this relationship. The cultural knowledge and community input is crucial to building a cultural deep world. This approach is also important as in many of these communities we want to build lasting and genuine relationships as opposed transactional relationships. In this understanding, it is the social and pedagogical outcomes of the process itself that benefit the community which are as important as the actual tangible output.

Contact with the community

I believe by far the most direct, and likely effective, way to involve community is to start with relationships you already have in the community and build upon those connections. I know of cases where students reach out to community organisations and encounter barriers because the students are not known by the community. This issue is not the case with all communities or organisations. However, there is a difficulty if you are trying to build a relationship and trust from zero as opposed to an already established relationship, however faint that relationship might be. Starting with relationships you already have can also provide you with further connections into the community. Your contacts are also best placed to point you in the right direction. The best approach might be to build these connections into longstanding and reciprocal relationships and always avoid treating them as transactional relationships. By starting with established relationships, you already have a direct and easier contact with the community.

However, there may be cases where the game designer or creator is outside the community and has no immediate contact with the community. If so, the first step is to reach out and contact someone from the community. Before you reach out there might be some questions you may consider, including:

- What is the name of the community or cultural group you wish to engage? This question might seem obvious, however, for example, you may wish to include local Indigenous cultures, but do not know the name of your local Indigenous community.
- What are the local council/government organisations or official representative bodies to contact? This question is especially important regarding Indigenous cultures and communities.
- If there are no government organisations or official representative bodies, are there any informal organisations or community groups to contact?
- If you are unable to find any organisations or community groups, are there alternative ways to find and contact the community (e.g. contacting local cultural institutions, government, etc.)?
- Do you know how to contact them?
- Are there any cultural protocols or special considerations involved in contacting the group?

In considering these questions, see Figure 5.4 for a flowchart of how to reach out and make contact with a community. This flow chart is based on the *Building relationships with local communities: Aboriginal and Torres Strait Islander*

COMMUNITY CONTACT FLOWCHART

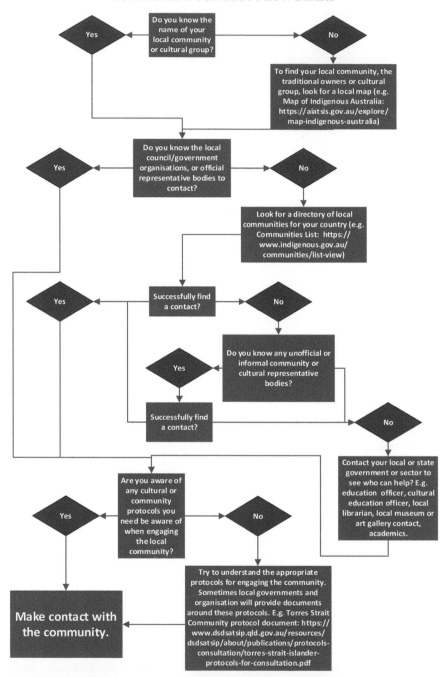

Figure 5.4 Community contact flow chart (Queensland Curriculum & Assessment Authroity, 2018) [graphical diagram]. Modified from *Building relationships with local communities: Aboriginal and Torres Strait Islander perspectives*, © State of Queensland (QCAA) 2018, licensed under CC BY 4.0.

perspectives document from the Queensland State Government in Australia (Queensland Curriculum & Assessment Authroity, 2018). This document aims at helping schools make contact with local Indigenous communities to facilitate forming relationships in order to then integrate local pedagogies into the classroom setting. The book's flowchart is a modified version of the Queensland Curriculum & Assessment Authority flow chart; however, it shifts the focus to community contact more broadly. However, the main premise of reaching out to contact the community to include in the process is the same in a game design project.

The flowchart for this book follows a similar approach for game project teams to contact the community they need to involve and cultural experts they may need to engage. The flowchart lays out a systematic approach to engaging the community and starts with finding the name of the community you wish to contact. This step might seem evident, but, for example, some designers might not know the name of their traditional Indigenous landowners or communities. I recommend searching the internet for reputable sources such as a government or organisational website that can provide a name of the community or cultural group you are looking for. I also recommend looking for reputable maps to find who might be the traditional owners of the land in your local area if you are trying to make contact with traditional owners.

Once you have established the name of the community you want to contact, you will need to find an organisation or representative body to contact. Again, a quick internet search can provide some starting points. Preferably you should try to contact an official representative body or organisation of that community. This contact could be a not-for-profit organisation, but it could also be a government body such as your local council, state government or possibly even national government. Being an official body may provide a better chance of reaching a representative community or senior figures in the community, although this is not always the case and will vary between organisation and communities.

If there are no official or government bodies available, you could try to find and contact an informal organisation or community group to engage. Once again, a quick internet search will be helpful in starting your journey. Informal community groups or bodies can still be very useful to reach smaller communities that do not have an official or government presence in your area. They are also useful to engage diaspora communities that might not be the traditional owners of the area where you live. However, these communities may lack the senior figures or only be representative of a portion of the community you wish to involve in the game development. These are only estimations, and each community and organisation will vary in size and representation.

If there are no identifiable informal community organisations from quick internet searches, you might be surprised to find that contacting local institutions such as your local government, librarian, museum and art gallery staff or academics might have contacts for your local community or for the community you wish to contact. Once you have your contact, you may wish to consider if there are any cultural or community protocols you need to be aware of when engaging the community. These protocols could be around speaking to certain members first, before approaching more senior members or practices and etiquette before, during and after the meeting. Once you have found your contact and are prepared, you can make contact and engage with the community to hopefully start a conversation.

Differing organisational structures, and community and kinship groups

Another important consideration that you should be aware of when engaging different communities and their representative organisations is how these organisations often operate. Some community organisations might operate fundamentally differently and may be structured in different ways to other organisations such as corporations. I recall a situation I heard from a friend. There was a senior engineer in a corporate firm who had to engage an Indigenous community because the company needed to access and use the land to carry out infrastructure work. The engineer went to a meeting with representatives from the community. The engineer was expecting to work out a solution between both parties for setting up the infrastructure within a few hours and then return back to the office to let management know what had been negotiated and arrange for a sign off on the agreement with the community. Once arriving at the meeting, the community representatives came to the discussions and listened to the proposal. However, at the end of the meeting nothing had been agreed to or even negotiated. The community representatives were to return to their community to further discuss the issue through a wide process of consultation and protocols. After which the community representatives would return again for further meetings as a part of a longer continual negotiation process.

In this story, there is a clear difference between the priorities of these organisations. One organisation is a corporate hierarchy with the main goal to make time-efficient and cost-effective decisions to move the process along within the project. The corporation has a clear hierarchy and reporting structure with certain members granted negotiating and decision-make privileges on behalf of the organisation. The other organisation is a land council or community group representing their people at the meeting and to listen to the proposal. Community organisations may have no clear hierarchy in this structure and instead decisions are made through discussion, deliberation and then consensus. The community organisation might have a nominated representative at the meeting, but they are not the sole decision maker and cannot decide or negotiate on the spot. Instead, the representative must return to the community to discuss the proposal with senior members and then and must engage with many more in the community before a decision can be made. There will likely be a back and forth between the different community members as each will have their own perspective on the decision to be made. After discussion a further meeting with the firm must be arranged with likely further dialogue to arrive at a decision between the corporate firm and the community organisation. Here, the process of coming together and discussing is just as important, if not more important, than the outcome itself. This consensual approach to decision-making can be the norm for many community group organisations and this needs to be considered when approaching and involving a community in participation.

Torres Strait culture – dances

Cultural dances are considered a central part of Torres Strait culture with dance used in ceremonies, significant cultural and personal events and some events for the public. Dances are almost always accompanied by singing and playing instruments, and holistically these dance music presentations often tell Torres Strait histories and stories.

Dance and hand movements align with the song's lyrics to signify different parts of the story or different events. Often dancers also wear cultural clothing, apparel and headwear while using hand ornaments and instruments during dances to aid the storytelling.

Dances will vary from island to island and the established dances that originate from the Torres Straits are still central to most dance presentations. However, as time progresses new elements and approaches are integrated into the body of knowledge of Torres Strait dance. Other cultures have influenced the types of dances in the Torres Strait. For example, some families perform the bamboo stick dance, handkerchief dance and fan dance, and these dances originate from Indonesia.

Another aspect that is a common feature of community-based organisations, especially when we consider Indigenous communities, is that these organisations are intertwined with familial and kinship structures. In some cases, these community organisations can be seen as a direct representation of the familial and kinship structures within the community and cultural group, especially if they are smaller localised communities. Many families might be on the same board or in the same organisation, but these representatives may be related to the entire community through one way or another. Those in the community organisation might link into other cultural institutions and experts such as cultural visual artists, performing artists in music and dance or other groups that have specific cultural knowledge. Because of these familial and kinship connections, community members can recognise and trace the connection of the relationships between each other even if they have met for the first time. In some cases, this allows one to have an initial opportunity and presents less barriers than an outsider approaching a community from the outside without any connection to the community.

For example, in TSVR, the Elder and I were trying to find cultural music to use at the beginning of the game and for the game trailer. We found a video clip of a Torres

Strait dance and music performance on the internet that the team thought worked well. We thought the rhythm fitted well with the game and wanted to use a section and sample a piece of the clip for use in the game. We located the company that performed in the video and we found the contact details for the manager. At that time, the Elder contacted the manager of the group and the manager was happy to let us use the music clip for the beginning of the game and trailer. Even though the Elder had never met the person before via phone or face-to-face, the Elder explained who he was and his family connections. The manager likely recognised the Elder through his last name, which is a common practice in the Torres Straits, and linked his place back to who she knew with the same surname and the Elder's place in the wider community. In this case, the Elder and the manager knew each other's families through Torres Strait familial and kinship ties even though they had never previously met.

In some cases, these connections with the community are built over generations. For example, my parents were posted to a remote Aboriginal community in the north of Australia. When we first met with the community, some community members asked my father if he knew Ted Loban and if he was Dato Ted's son. My father said that Dato Ted was his uncle. Many of the community members had known Dato Ted because in the past the church boat would take pregnant women and their families from the community to Waiben. At that time, travelling to Waiben by boat was the closest medical facility for the women to give birth as the wet season cut off any road connections to the community. Dato Ted used to help families coming from the community and many people from this community remembered this support. Even before Dato Ted, Great Dato Tom Loban also helped Aboriginal people along the shoreline of Cape York Peninsula who needed food and shelter. These kinship connections were important because they provided my parents, who were working in the community, a solid and amicable foundation upon which to build a relationship with the community. In remote communities where the entire town know each other, positive and friendly relationship are particularly important to gain community support around local matters and initiatives. Therefore, some relationships with community can take generations to build the good will with the community. This example highlights the importance of kinship connections and embedding a community member in your project team, particularly if you need to engage and involve the wider community.

Linking into these structures typically comes with the spirit of reciprocity and that potentially in the future you will work and give back to the community in a similar way that you received help. These are not a one-way transactional relationship and are instead relationships and connections within a community that build over time through various interactions and relationships. For this reason, community participation, especially from the beginning of the project, is so crucial to the project. Not only can community members provide deep insights and perspectives of culture, but often there are connections into the community to help facilitate and streamline further engagement with the wider community. We need to engage with these communities in the spirit of reciprocity as this approach is how long-standing relationships are built and not necessarily through seeking some sort of strategic benefit or immediate gain.

Conclusion

There are various approaches to involve the community in the creation of a game design process. These approaches can range from embedding community members into the game design team to consulting specific cultural experts to having a more generalised approach of involving a wider section of the community especially in the playtest or quality assurance process. These approaches are all valid methods to involve community and you may even wish to implement several approaches in your game design project to further embed cultural perspectives into the game design. These approaches also provide the opportunity to give back to the community such as providing opportunities for those from the community to tell their stories and obtain new skillsets. You must also be aware of the organisational structure of community groups which can affect how the organisations respond to decisions, the decision-making process and their priorities.

The key is that you involve the community in the representation of their own culture in games. Having more and different forms of community participation could provide more diverse and deeper cultural input into the game design and the cultural representations in the resulting game. Hopefully these representations are not only culturally sound, as to not offend or misrepresent, but also possibly advocate for and address cultural and community perspectives and issues respectively. For many real reciprocal relationships, you may very well be returning to the community long after the project or research has finished. Participation of the community is by far the most direct and the most effective method to integrate culture into game design; however, there are other methods to access and bring cultural understandings into game design such as through cultural immersion by the designer and rigorous research.

References

Adrenalin Games and Metia Interactive. (2017). *Māori Pā Wars* [video game]. Adrenalin Games.

Antariksha Sanchar. (2022). *Antariksha Sanchar*. http://www.antariksha.in/.

Beat Games. (2018). *Beat Saber* [video game].

Brayboy, B. M., Gough, H. R., Leonard, B., Roehl, R., & Solyom, J. A. (2012). Reclaiming scholarship: Critical indigenous research methodologies. In S. D. Lapan, M. L. T. Quartoli, & F. J. Riemer (Eds.), *Qualitative research: An introduction to methods and designs* (pp. 423–450). Jossey-Bass.

Castellano, M. B. (2014). Ethics of aboriginal research. In W. Teays, J.-S. Gordon, & A. Dundes Renteln (Eds.), *Global bioethics and human rights: Contemporary issues* (pp. 273–288). Rowman & Littlefield.

Feldman, S. (2005). Quality assurance: Much more than testing. *Queue, 3*(1), 26–29.

Greer, S. (2010). Heritage and empowerment: Community-based Indigenous cultural heritage in northern Australia. *International Journal of Heritage Studies, 16*(1-2), 45–58.

Harding, S. (2015). Objectivity and diversity. In *Objectivity and diversity*. University of Chicago Press.

Kapur, M. (2008). Productive failure. *Cognition and Instruction, 26*(3), 379–424.

Kultima, A. (2015). *Defining game jam*. FDG.

Laiti, O. (2021). *Old ways of knowing, new ways of playing—the potential of collaborative game design to empower Indigenous Sámi* [Dissertation thesis]. University of Lapland.

Laiti, O., Harrer, S., Uusiautti, S., & Kultima, A. (2020). Sustaining intangible heritage through video game storytelling-the case of the Sami game jam. *International Journal of Heritage Studies*, *27*(3), 296–311.

LaPensée, E. (2011). *Survivance* [game].

LaPensée, E. (2014). Survivance as an indigenously determined game. *AlterNative: An International Journal of Indigenous Peoples*, *10*(3), 263–275.

LaPensée, E. (2017). *Thunderbird strike* [video game].

LaPensée, E. (2020). SPEAR: A framework for Indigenous cultural games. *ANTARES: Letras e Humanidades*, *12*(28), 4–22.

LaPensée, E. A., Laiti, O., & Longboat, M. (2022). Towards sovereign games. *Games and Culture*, *17*(3), 328–343.

Lucashenko, M. (2015). The first Australian democracy. *Meanjin*, *74*(3), 7.

Mancini, H. (2018). Mā te rongo ka mohio: Māori Pā wars and Kaupapa Māori methodology at the interface of video games. *Back Story Journal of New Zealand Art, Media & Design History*, (5), 71–85. https://doi.org/10.24135/backstory.vi5.38

Nodding Heads Games. (2020). *Raji: An ancient epic* [video game]. SuperGG.com

Ong, Y., Loban, R. D., & Parrila, R. K. (2022). The fight is the dance: Modding Chinese martial arts and culture into beat saber. *Journal of Games Criticism*, *5*(A), X–X.

Parkinson, C., & Jones, T. (2019). Aboriginal people's aspirations and the Australian curriculum: A critical analysis. *Educational Research for Policy and Practice*, *18*(1), 75–97.

Pinnguaq. (2016). *Honour water* [video game]. https://apps.apple.com/app/id1146954514

Queensland Curriculum & Assessment Authroity. (2018). *Building relationships with local communities: Aboriginal and Torres Strait Islander perspectives*. https://www.qcaa.qld.edu.au/downloads/approach2/indigenous_build_relationship.pdf

Queensland Department of Aboriginal and Torres Strait Islander Policy and Development. (2000). *Mina Mir Lo Ailan Mun*. Department of Aboriginal & Torres Strait Islander Policy and Development.

Salen, K., Tekinbaş, K. S., & Zimmerman, E. (2004). *Rules of play: Game design fundamentals*. MIT press.

Smith, L. T. (1999). *Decolonizing methodologies: Research and indigenous peoples*. Zed books.

Smith, L. T. (2015). *Kaupapa Māori research-some kaupapa Māori principles*. In L. Pihama & K. South (Eds.), *Kaupapa Rangahau A reader: A collection of readings from the Kaupapa Maori Research Workshop Series Led* (pp. 46–52). Te Kotahi Research Institute.

Sykes, J., & Federoff, M. (2006). *Player-centred game design. CHI'06 extended abstracts on Human factors in computing systems* (pp. 1731–1734). Association for Computing Machinery. https://doi.org/10.1145/1125451.1125774

The Indian Land Tenure Foundation. (2019). *When rivers were trails* [video game].

Zeiler, X., & Mukherjee, S. (2022). Video game development in India: A cultural and creative industry embracing regional cultural heritage(s). *Games and Culture*. https://doi.org/10.1177/15554120211045143

Interlude

The Tombstone Opening

Remarks from Gehamat Loban

Figure 5.5 My father helping unveil my Dato's, Frank Loban's, Tombstone with my
great Dato watching on at the Tombstone Opening [photograph]. Year: Circa
1963–1964.

On the day of the Tombstone Opening, the priest will say a prayer and open the ceremony. Often, the priest will be from the islands and understand the practices and
know the family. The priest we know well is Anglican, but the spiritual ceremony
facilitator could vary depending on the denomination and religion of the deceased.
Once the ceremony has opened, family members and other distant relatives can begin to unravel the cloth around the Tombstone. As we unveil the tombstone, we re-
veal under the cloth all sorts of objects. There could be money, island artefacts such
as Warups, mats, spears, Waps and so on. We share the money and objects under
the Tombstone cloth among family members who unravelled the cloth. Typically,

DOI: 10.1201/9781003276289-8

those who unveil the Tombstone receive the money or items within the cloth. Once the cloth has been unravelled and the Tombstone unveiled, we go to the hall for the feast. See Figure 5.5 for a photograph of my Dato's Tombstone Opening.

On the day of the Tombstone Opening, we take the cooked meals to the hall or eating place. If required, we reheat any food that needs heating before serving. We monitor the food carefully to ensure it has not spoiled. Monitoring is especially important for us as organisers, as our reputation in the community can be at stake. This concern is especially important within a close-knit island community like ours. The event is all about honouring the family member. To honour the deceased, we present the best event we can, give the best we can and allow our guests to enjoy themselves. We will call certain people to eat first such as the Elderly and immediate family members of the deceased and others close to the deceased. We often seat adults and children separately depending on the number of people and for serving purposes. We could have several seatings with different people eating at different times. Those who have been serving the food and working at the event eat after everyone else has been looked after. Once we have all eaten, the entertainment and dancing can begin. This event is a happy time because the community has come together, and it symbolises the end of the mourning period.

Once the eating and entertainment have finished, we then begin to clean up the kitchen, the hall and all the crockery, cutlery and saucepans. We need to stack the chairs and sweep the hall. Sometimes, the hall is used for church on Sunday, which may be the next day. The next day, we need to distribute all the cleaned crockery, cutlery and saucepans back to the owners. This part of the event is also a wind-down time, where the organisers can relax as the main event is finished.

We create packages of any leftover bags of rice or other foods and give the bags to those who helped at the Tombstone Opening with the organisation, catering and cleaning. Sometimes, we take these packages to contributors, even those who are located on other islands, which means we will have to travel over in a dinghy to drop off the package. This practice feeds into the spirit of sharing and reciprocity of the event. These events help reinforce strongly forged family and community ties that develop respect, reciprocity and obligation throughout the process. In the community, we respect others even more when they contribute and fulfil their obligations, but even if they do not, we still have to show respect. This notion of respect is also an everyday practice in the Island world and not just for the Tombstone Opening.

6 Cultural immersion, rigorous research and ethics in game design

Community participation throughout the game design process is the most direct and preferred method to access deep culture. However, there are additional methods that can be used to support community participation and to improve our understanding of the culture. This chapter is dedicated to briefly exploring two other methods: cultural immersion and rigorous research. The chapter also covers a brief exploration of the ethics of embedding culture into video games and game design, particularly for outsiders to the culture. Designers should use all the methods available to facilitate embedding deep and genuine cultural depictions in-game, but the decision to do so is an ethical decision for designers to make depending on their own context.

Direct experience and immersion are methods to support the designer's understanding of the community and gain greater familiarity with the culture. Dewey (1986) places emphasis on learning by doing and the intimate connection between education and personal experience. If we were to engage directly with the community ourselves and be a part of that community and cultural setting, we would be gaining our own firsthand experiences as opposed to indirect interpretations from other sources (e.g. books). Of course, these cultural experiences are still interpreted through our own cultural lens (e.g. an outsider visiting Indonesia does not have an Indonesian experience but rather a foreigner's experience of Indonesia); however, these experiences and the immersions allow us to make sense of and reflect on the culture on our own terms. Obviously, the experience by itself is only useful if we enter into these situations with an awareness of our own biases and attempt to have an open and non-judgmental mindset where possible (Doerr, 2013; Tan, 2012). Afterwards, we can reflect and try to better understand our experiences as part of this learning process. It is also important to be aware that our own experiences are likely not as insightful as the lifelong experiences of those in the community or forming lifelong relationships with those in the community. Nonetheless, we have to begin our learning journey somewhere, and these direct experiences of cultural immersion provide greater connection and possibly more meaningful insight than the multiple second- and third-hand interpretations by others (e.g. such as through books). The central idea here is that, through cultural immersion, designers can obtain these experiences themselves and can more confidently make sense of such experiences when discussed by the community and when designing

DOI: 10.1201/9781003276289-9

their worlds. Even if those experiences of the culture are tainted by their own cultural understandings, designers have some level of firsthand experience.

Torres Strait story – Kupas

Kupas is a talking sand crab who appears in the story of Gelam, the man from Moa (Gela, 1993). He is a benevolent figure who shelters Gelam and his mother from the Dogai, who is searching for them. He protects Gelam and his mother and blinds the Dogai. In Torres Strait Virtual Reality (TSVR), he can be spotted on Buru where he has hunted Dogais.

Greater understanding through cultural immersion and experience

There has been diverse research from multiple disciplines to support learning through cultural immersion and lived experience. In the study by Gallagher et al. (2019), they discuss how groups of students from various health professions participated in a Māori Interprofessional programme in New Zealand. Discussions from the focus groups of the students and analysis by Gallagher et al. (2019) indicated that the programme was positively regarded and even transformative for the individuals involved. Students reported that the "lived experience" in the communities built upon their own understandings of the community and, in many cases, extended their prior learnings of Indigenous health. For the students, working, learning and living in the Māori context was a direct and immersive experience. This approach was not theoretical learning in a classroom, but rather a lived experience within the community that was steeped in culture.

In another study, Gainsford and Robertson (2019) discuss how engagement with Wiradyuri Elders in Australia while on Country (traditional Indigenous lands) was used as learning through immersion for law students and the lecturer. The lecturer and students found that the Elders' storytelling was a valuable and legitimate tool of critical analysis of cultural and historical connection to the land. In the three-day immersion programme, law students listened to Elders tell their story and explain their connections to the land and the meaning of the land to them. The experience exposed students to new perspectives and the historical wrongs wrought against the Wiradyuri community. For one student in particular, they had not fully comprehended the concepts promoted during class in the university course. However, through the cultural immersion programme, the theoretical concepts discussed in class made sense through the Elder storytelling and being on Country. Concepts such as legal pluralism, Aboriginal sovereignty, reconciliation, self-determination and land rights now had real meaning that could be backed up and communicated through lived experiences and being on the land.

In another study, Burgess (2019) focused on a cultural immersion and training programme for local communities and schools that was run by the local Aboriginal cultural knowledge holders. Data from both questionnaires and interviews indicated the significant impact this cultural immersion and training programme had on teachers' learnings about their local area. The programme also challenged the assumptions of the teachers and prompted them to reflect on their own classroom pedagogies and content about Indigenous Australia. Based on the results, Burgess (2019) recommends that Indigenous knowledge holders be the ones to lead the programmes of cultural education for the most impact. As previously discussed, the most impactful and effective learning of a culture occurs through a firsthand experience.

Torres Strait story – Kuiam

Kuiam's story originates from Mabuyag, but he seems to be known through several parts of the Torres Straits. Kuiam was a warrior of great martial prowess; however, he was also able to command magic, which he inherited from his father. Instead of using the traditional weapons such as the long bow and mace of the Torres Straits, Kuiam fought with a spear and a Woomera (a device that augments a spear's speed and impact). These weapons were handed down by his father, who was an Aboriginal person from the mainland. Kuiam does not feature in TSVR, but is still an important Torres Strait figure nonetheless.

In the context of the Americas, Thibeault (2019) examines the experience of social work students who spent three days working with the Lakota community. The students engaged in cultural and day-to-day activities, including rebuilding a women's Inipi (Lakota for sweat lodge). Students learned from a Lakota Elder about the community and traditions, and cultural appropriateness within the community. Some of the students also took part in a sweat lodge ceremony, while other students engaged in other cultural practices such as preparing food and making crafts. Establishing a relationship with the community is important prior to entry into a community and helps ensure the community's needs and requirements are being met. In this way, the students are spending time in the community and assisting the community to build meaningful relationships rather than a practice of "doing it or fixing it". These are acts of cultural exchange, reciprocity and relationships.

Building genuine and non-transactional relationships where possible with the community is highly important, as Doerr (2013) cautions against just learning about another culture. Only learning about a culture without any of the relationships can instil a self vs. other approach to learning about different cultures and communities. Instead, Doerr (2013) prompts us to think about the individuals we meet from the community as well as our own different backgrounds. Our backgrounds are intersections of social, economic, cultural and political situations that affect us all as individuals in the community. This approach not only emphasises learning from people and knowing how they live, but also aims to avoid essentialising or stereotyping them based on only a culturally focused engagement. In this way, learning about the community and the place where people live is important because these are real interactions with real people.

Cultural immersion is insightful for those attempting to better understand the community through face-to-face interaction. However, immersion by an outsider may not fully represent the true circumstances of people within the community, and it is important to be wary of the limitations as well as the affordances of your position as an outsider as well as other social, economic and political factors as pointed out by Doerr (2013). In a personal example, my first memories were during the mid-1990s in a remote Aboriginal community. The bread sold at the local store was exorbitantly overpriced and always mouldy. So, my parents, not wanting to eat mouldy bread, bought a bread-maker so we would have fresh bread. However, to obtain the bread-maker at that time required certain knowledge, skills and wealth to locate, order, purchase and use the bread-maker. Bread-makers were not readily available in the remote community with little outside access. In this scenario, there are not only cultural differences that influence one's perspective, but also differences around knowledge, skills and wealth that were brought from outside the community to help us and changed our experience of our time within the community. Although we can be immersed in the community for a period of time, there can still be fundamental differences in the way we live even inside the community and our experiences of that place are not necessarily a true reflection of the community experience.

While we can live in the community and even be accepted by the community, there are still other factors that limit our understanding and perspective within the community. However, in some cases, outsider observations can provide insights that might not be apparent to the community or seen as a given in the community. Such observations may also not be present in materials such as a written book. Cultural immersion provides this unique perspective that may not be evident to community members or through your own non-experiential research. However, again, our outside view typically does not have complete knowledge or a full perspective. Therefore, fundamentally, we should still seek to understand community perspectives and their perspective of the world while still being aware of our own influencing biases during a cultural immersion.

Immersive and face-to-face interactions can allow participants different avenues for learning other than through cognition, such as through affect (i.e. emotion-based pedagogy). One example of research by Harrison and Clarke (2022), while not specifically related to experiences of culture, involved students exposed to a speaker of the Stolen Generations who talked about his life growing up (Harrison & Clarke, 2022). Students heard this speaker and listened to his narration of the trauma he was exposed to throughout his childhood in various foster homes. The students expressed and discussed their physical responses, such as numbness, and emotional reactions, such as sadness and anger. However, anonymously, a number of these students raised and explained that they had faced similar trauma themselves. In this way, these students were not necessarily responding to only the rational and informational exposure of the recount of the traumatic experience. Instead, the students were making sense of these traumatic experiences through affective learning in conjunction with their own lived trauma and exposure to traumatic experiences in their own lives. In this way, some of the audience were understanding and making sense of this oration through their own experiences, which prompted a form of emotion-based learning and sensorial experiences, which act as a powerful stimulus for learning beyond cognition. Although learning through shared traumatic experiences and emotions is an extreme example, when we consider culture immersion, these experiences may prompt emotions and sensorial input, opening up different avenues for learning such as through affect.

Collectively, immersion in communities provides impactful and effective learning experiences about a culture. One can read a book or view a video; however, many of the concepts communicated may not come to life or be apparent until you experience them for yourself. These subtleties and nuances of the culture occur through real experiences with the community and allow for a better shot at understanding the deeper culture. During the process, we should also be aware of our own community's position and biases and how these factors can influence our cultural immersion. Immersion also allows for access to other avenues of learning, such as through affect. However, meaningful cultural immersion usually takes a significant amount of time in the community, as even very short immersion programmes tend to be over several days (Pope-Davis et al., 1997). In this approach, we should try to prioritise meaningful relationships with the community over transactional ones within the project. Another excellent experiential and cultural immersion approach for learning about a community and culture is the learning from Country/Place method (Harrison & Skrebneva, 2020).

Learning from Country/Place

Learning from Country/Place was developed within an educational context with the aim of assisting teachers to embed Indigenous knowledge into the classroom (Harrison & Skrebneva, 2020). Learning from Country/Place addresses the same fundamental problem that we are dealing with here in regard to culture and game design. Namely, how can we embed Indigenous (or more generally, cultural) knowledge in the classroom (or a game) without creating misrepresentations? The concept of Country/Place is a key concept in the lives of many Indigenous people in Australia. This approach was intended to assist teachers in articulating Indigenous knowledge to their own students.

Learning from Country/Place evaluates not only school learning outcomes in a national assessment by the education system, but also the connections to community and parents and students' connection to community. For Harrison and Skrebneva (2020), Country/Place is the medium through which all students can learn about Aboriginal and Torres Strait Islander people. Country/Place is representative of the worldview and ontologies of many Indigenous Australians. Country/Place is often seen as the physical environment of the local area; however, for many Indigenous people, it is much more and is also a representation of the people and their connections to the land. Engagements and learnings from Country/Place and the community could also be present in sensorial and affective forms of learning where cognition is not always required. Some Indigenous people derive their cultures and knowledge from this deep and intimate connection between themselves and their

Country or Place. Similar ideas are discussed by other authors (Bhardwaj, 1983; Eck, 2012; Singh, 2020) with the concepts of a cultural and religious/sacred geography and site-based folklore used to show the intimate connection between the people, the landscape and seascape and the culture or religion.

In the research by Rey and Harrison (2018), they discuss honouring country and community by Learning from Country/Place in the form of various activities. One activity was centred around painting the cultural connection to the land. Another activity was an excursion to the botanical garden and Ku-ring-gai National Park in Australia to learn about local community connections to the land and the medicinal use of plants from the area. These activities were facilitated by Elders and cultural knowledge holders with deep connections to Country/Place. In this way, the Learning from Country/Place approach urges the learner to avoid learning about Indigenous people from inside a classroom, most of which could be considered second-hand knowledge and, in many cases, a theoretical rather than an experiential understanding.

However, it should be noted that in Australia many Indigenous people have been historically, and often violently, displaced or, in more recent times, required to move to other parts of the nation for employment or work opportunities. Although Learning from Country/Place is highly valuable for learning about some local people, the approach needs to be applied differently when approaching cultures that do not have longstanding and significant connections to the land in the same way. These cultural practices and communities can remain strong even for those living outside their homelands. However, the experiential pedagogical approach might look different, as direct interaction with the land to understand culture might not be viable with some communities. For example, I could still teach about Torres Strait culture through traditional palm leaf weaving outside of the Torres Straits, but I might use a substitute for the palm leaves and explain the importance of the palm in more depth. The direct harvesting of palm fronds from the palm and interaction with the landscape are not available, but the weaving practice and coordinated activity with others can still take place. Regardless, meaningful learning tends to be direct experiences and interactions with community and learning through immersion in the culture.

These cultural immersion experiences are possibly the best opportunity for you to understand the community and culture yourself. However, these experiences alone do not guarantee that you will understand the community or culture in any meaningful way. It is possible for someone to live in a community and cultural setting, but still have no respect for or deep understanding of that culture at all. Indeed, some people might have strong or even intimate relationships with people from the culture or community, but still do not respect the culture or have any deep understanding of the people or culture. Therefore, an open ethos and non-judgmental approach are helpful to attain a greater understanding of the culture, where you do not impose your own judgments on the people (Tan, 2012). These experiences might also need further reflection to make sense of their meaning. An open and non-judgmental approach to culture does not guarantee that you will acquire a complete knowledge of the deep culture and attain a full perspective of the community. However, this approach does open the possibility of a deeper understanding of the community and their perspectives. While firsthand experiences are not always possible in the game designing process, the designer may wish to supplement cultural immersion experiences with additional research. In these cases, you can engage in rigorous research with various resources and materials.

Torres Strait art – beading and island apparel

Bead necklaces, bracelets and other apparel are common in the Torres Straits and have long been a part of Torres Strait fashion.

Bead necklaces and bracelets for arms were a part of precolonial fashion and were made from a variety of materials. Materials used in beaded apparel could have included different seeds (gidi gidi beads), shells, pearls, etc. However, one of the more common materials used both today and historically is beads, especially glass beads.

Today, glass bead apparel is common in Torres Strait fashion. The apparel is often very colourful and can have simple or highly complex patterns. The bead patterns can reflect the islands, personal relations, religion or other cultural aspects of the Torres Straits. Often, they are used as everyday wear by some Island people. See Figure 6.1 for three examples of strand patterns.

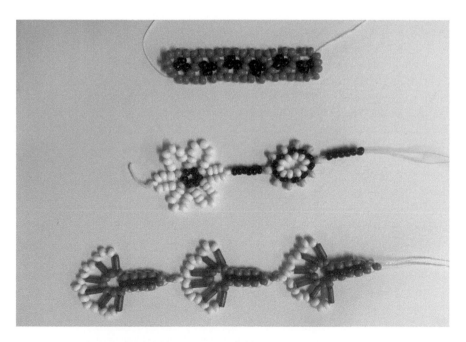

Figure 6.1 Three examples of different stranded bead patterns used for bracelets and necklaces [photograph].

Rigorous research

The preferred approach to gaining insight into community and culture should be to engage those in the community and then learn from the community through cultural immersion approaches, such as Learning from Country/Place. However, certain places and communities may be less accessible, or you may wish to further support these experiences with your own research on the community. This additional rigorous research with different materials could be in the form of books, journal articles, videos, podcasts, various websites and more. Such research can either reconfirm your understanding and engagement with the community or could be at odds, in which case you may need to assess what information is more culturally appropriate. However, while conducting research to supplement your community participation, you will need to be careful about your choice of research materials as not all resources are created equal.

All materials are to some degree tainted by the authors' and consumers' own cultural lens, and are open to reinterpretations and re-representations within their own minds. However, in the process of game designing with culture and building our game worlds, we need a practical way to distinguish between the credibility of the materials in relation to the representation of the community and culture. For example, a book written by a community member in conjunction with the community over several years and supported by rigorous research is far more likely to be credible and insightful than a website constructed by an outsider of the community in a week with only second- or third-hand sources. In a similar vein to the palm and the Dogai, some materials could be more superficial or have misleading representations while others have undergone a deeper and rigorous process of production. Therefore, you will need to differentiate between credible and less credible resources to support your cultural and community-based game design.

To support your selection and evaluation of various research materials, we can use the *Selecting and evaluating resources* document from the Queensland Studies Authority (2007) in Australia. This government document is intended for teachers to use when they are developing school-based resources or selecting materials for their own classroom. It was designed for teachers in Queensland, Australia; however, the resource can be used nationwide throughout Australia by teachers. While most of the criteria discussed in the document are applicable to Indigenous Australians, many of the criteria may also be applied to the research with other cultural groups more generally. The criteria are relatively blunt in the form of a table, and the issues raised in the criteria may not be applicable to all materials. Indeed, some materials that you find might still be useful or hold some insight, but not necessarily meet all the criteria. Therefore, these criteria might be more useful for raising your own awareness to different issues with materials and for being cautious if you are engaging with materials you are unsure about in regards to the community. Nonetheless, the criteria do provide general indicators of issues to be aware of when searching for and evaluating materials to inform your cultural world building.

The *Selecting and evaluating resources* (Queensland Studies Authority, 2007) document outlines several criteria for evaluating and selecting culturally appropriate resources. However, I have condensed and revised the criteria to reflect a more generalised culture and community approach. The criteria tend to fall into a number of categories:

- Reliability
- A balanced nature of presentation
- Community participation and support

Reliability

As discussed by Said (1978), in the past and even today, many materials depicting different communities have often contained stereotypes and highly generalised depictions. These depictions of various people are often taken from the perspective of an outside observer. These generalisations may be using the practice of one group and attributing it to many people (e.g. a generalisation is that all Indigenous Australians engage in dot painting). In some instances, materials may be out of date, have omissions and distortions of/around the truth and fail to acknowledge the diversity of different cultural groups. In some cases, the observers' biases have also influenced what they saw and how they saw the community. We have to be aware of potential issues with some sources and assess the reliability of the materials, especially in discussions of culture and community. Therefore, we also want to be sure that the materials are reliable in relation to any knowledge, discussion or representations of the culture or community in question. See Table 6.1 for related questions, indicators and possible actions for reliability issues.

A balanced nature of presentation

Within both Aboriginal and Torres Strait Islander cultures in Australia, there is significant diversity and complexity. This diversity might also be the case for many other communities and cultures around the globe that you may work with in your project. When depicting or discussing these communities, it is important to present a balanced portrayal of the different societies and cultures. Be wary of materials that exaggerate or prejudicially comment on aspects of the community, especially if you are recreating deep representations. See Table 6.2 for related questions, indicators and possible actions for a balanced nature of presentation issues.

Community participation and support

As strongly advocated in this book, input and participation from the community are key. This approach is also the case with materials that you might use when designing your game. Material developed by the community or with their input tends to provide deeper insight into the culture. See Table 6.3 for related questions, indicators and possible actions for genuineness issues.

Table 6.1 Reliability issues, related questions, indicators and actions (Queensland Studies Authority, 2007)

Issue	Questions	Indicators	Action
Older materials	Is the material up to date? If not, who is the author?	Publication date of the materials. Although older materials might seem more reliable and close to the original source, they could also be published by outsiders from the community and may have little input from the community themselves. While this issue is not always the case, do consider newer materials that might have more up-to-date information and balanced perspectives	Look for newer books where applicable, or when using older materials, examine and assess the authorship
Truthful materials	Is the material truthful and forthcoming?	Some books may omit or distort details. Some of these issues are easy to spot, while sometimes they are not. For example, there is a common falsehood that Tasmanian Aboriginal people no longer exist, which is demonstrably untrue	Approach local communities about their history and to find suitable materials
Terra Nullius	Does the material perpetuate the concept of Terra Nullius?	Statements such as "a vast and empty land" and "explorers discovering vast tracts of unused land". These ideas also feed into Indigenous people not properly making use of the land or living there to begin with	Avoid using the materials in your research where possible
Indigenous resistance to invasion and colonisation	Does the material ignore or misrepresent Indigenous resistance to foreign invasion, occupation and colonisation?	In some cases, invading and/or colonising nations engaging in violent land theft are painted as deserving to take land while the victims are painted as not properly utilising the land and deserving of being displaced into camps or killed Indigenous people are often not portrayed as being defenders of the land and instead are framed as treacherous, murderous and attacking peaceful colonisers These kinds of materials are lopsided and perpetuate only one side of the history, specifically that of the perpetrator and nation taking hostile actions	Avoid using materials that portray communities, especially Indigenous communities, in this biased way

(Continued)

Table 6.1 (Continued)

Issue	Questions	Indicators	Action
Stereotypes and generalisations	Does the material stereotype or generalise the culture or community in question?	Sweeping statements that imply practices apply to all communities and groups: "The Aboriginal people play the didgeridoo" or "The Aboriginal people were nomadic"	Avoid using these over-generalised materials as the validity of such statements are questionable and possibly false
Diversity among cultural groups	Is diversity within different cultures and languages ignored?	Materials which discuss "The Aboriginal Language" or "The Asian philosophy and religion" tend to ignore the diversity of these communities. There are many kinds of Aboriginal Australian languages and various kinds of philosophies and religions in Asia. These statements tend to homogenise these different groups	Perhaps focus on materials that have more specificity and detail on specific community and groups
Caricatures	Does the visual depiction of the culture or community represent or create caricature?	The visual depictions evoke caricatures of the culture and community. The visual depictions are intrusive, demeaning and reinforce negative stereotypes. In some cases, the illustrations may not match the text	Aim to use resources that convey a fair and positive depictions of the culture. Exceptions might be where you are using the caricatures to point out examples of stereotypes or racism Be aware that the visual depictions should match the text
Visuals and details	Does the written material explain the visual materials?	For example, does the captions of a picture explain in detail the specifics of the people and culture? Is the material left open for consumers to make guesses or assumption? For example, does it include their names, communities, location, time, etc.?	Looks for materials with more details and specifics where possible to provide a fuller understanding

Modified from *Selecting and evaluating resources,* © State of Queensland (QCAA) 2007, licensed under CC BY 4.0.

Table 6.2 Balanced nature of presentation issues, related questions, indicators and actions (Queensland Studies Authority, 2007)

Issue	Questions	Indicators	Action
Gender representation	Is one gender overrepresented in the material or in inappropriate places?	Some materials can over emphasise the importance of one gender's role more than the other in different cultural practices (e.g. food gathering or ceremonies)	Find materials with a more balanced view
Trivialises the culture or roles in society	Does the material trivialise one gender's roles in the society?	In the past, some materials imply that one gender's tasks are more onerous and trivialise the importance of other gender roles (e.g. male's tasks are more important than women's tasks)	Avoid using the materials where possible and try to find materials that present the roles and perspectives of both genders
Racist overtones and undertones	Are stereotyping and racist connotations present?	Materials that suggest the cultural group or community are "backwards". Phrases about technology "simple tools and weapons". Derogatory terms to describe a community or culture Biases of the author might be seen in descriptions such as the "brave settlers" and "treacherous blacks". Negative connotations when referring to education, lifestyles, technology and transmission of information; e.g. "The Aboriginal people had no tradition of reading and writing" or "Life was a constant search for food"	Avoid using the materials where possible
Western or Eurocentric assumptions of audience	Does the resource exclude some readers by assuming a Western or European background?	The materials suggest the readers ancestors came from a colder climate and unlike "us". It assumes the audience are mostly of European ancestry and not from other heritages around the world. These might tend to read older books	Use with caution

(Continued)

Table 6.2 (Continued)

Issue	Questions	Indicators	Action
Excludes Torres Strait Islander people (Australia specifically)	Does the resource exclude Torres Strait Islander people?	In some resources, there is a tendency to only focus on Aboriginal people as Australia's only Indigenous people. However, there are two Indigenous people in Australia: Torres Strait Islanders and Aboriginal people	Look for materials that also reflect Torres Strait Islander and Aboriginal people in discussions about Indigenous Australians generally. Materials about specific clans or communities are fine if there are in-depth discussions about a specific group
Exoticisation (Orientalism)	Do the materials emphasise the "exotic" aspects of the culture to the exclusion of other cultural aspects?	In some materials, there can be an over-emphasis on initiation rites, different ceremonies, body ornamentation, etc. The exoticisation and focus on specific aspects of a culture have been previously discussed by Said (1978)	Look for more balanced materials on cultural practices and aspects
Portrayal of culture and people as living in the past or not changing	Do the materials assume that all the community or people from a particular culture still live in the past?	Some materials only focus on the historical cultural practices, or a view of the community as only existing in history. This point is primarily an issue if the game premise is to be set in a contemporary setting. For example, the sole focus on historical art form to the exclusion of present-day artists or contemporary interpretations of cultural art. The focus on historical depictions in materials can paint the picture in the mind of the consumer that the culture is either no longer existent or continues to live as they did historically, which is often not true	Be aware of this material, especially if the intended game setting is in a contemporary setting. Continue the approach to involve community participation in the project as well as your own cultural immersion

Table 6.3 Community participation and support issues, related questions, indicators and actions (Queensland Studies Authority, 2007)

Issue	Questions	Indicators	Action
Acknowledgment of community participation and willingness in the development of the materials	Do the materials acknowledge community participation in the development processes of the materials?	Names of people from the community who helped create the resource. There might be specific references to community groups that contributed to the material's development, e.g. Torres Strait Regional Authority, Mura Kosker Sorority, etc.	Look for acknowledgements of involvement and endorsement
Community authorship	Is the author of the materials from the community?	Culture-related materials that involve an author from the community often clearly advise the reader of the author's identity and their cultural background	Look for information about the author either in the materials itself or via other research (e.g. a quick internet search). Community authorship is the preferred material to use. However, in some cases, authorship from someone in the community does not always guarantee the materials will be complete, as the materials may only be part of the knowledge or from one perspective in the community
Information about secret or sacred practices, items or representations	Does the material present information about secret and/or sacred items, practices, sites and representations?	Materials that present sacred or private ceremonies and rites, for example, some women's or men's initiation rites. Some materials presenting specific sites, e.g. sacred sites of particular groups. For certain groups, materials detailing the processes involved in Indigenous ceremonies and practices may not have been appropriately disclosed. For some communities, knowledge is relational and often kept within a community	Do not use the materials without first discussing with local community Consult with the local community for examples that are appropriate for use

(Continued)

Table 6.3 (Continued)

Issue	Questions	Indicators	Action
		Depending on the community, inclusion of photographs and names of deceased Torres Strait Islander and/or Aboriginal people may or may not be appropriate Some photographs and textual details are significant to specific Aboriginal and/or Torres Strait Islander groups, e.g. some information is not appropriate to be viewed by members outside the community	
Materials about the local area	Is the material about your local area?	Supporting statements or endorsements by local, regional or state community group	Check with your local community
Local, regional or national endorsement by community or culture	Has the material been endorsed by any official local, regional, state or territory, or national community group?	Acknowledgments to show that the book has been endorsed by an official community group. An acknowledgement of community participation in the development or production	You can consider using the materials If still unsure, check with the community
Material endorsed by cultural group or community	Has the material been endorsed by other informal community groups?	A statement from a person or informal group from the community. An acknowledgement of community participation in the development or production	You can consider using the materials If still unsure, check with the community

Modified from *Selecting and evaluating resources,* © State of Queensland (QCAA) 2007, licensed under CC BY 4.0.

Ethics of cultural representation, game design and monetisation

In discussions of cultural representations in video games, the idea of cultural appropriation arises. Cultural appropriation is "the active 'making one's own' of another culture's elements" (Rogers, 2006, p. 476). However, some forms of cultural appropriation might vary from a more equal and innocent cultural exchange between different communities to more malicious cultural exploitation or domination (Rogers, 2006). In this way, not all cultural exchanges are equal, and factors such as the power of one cultural dominance over another need to be considered

(Arya, 2021). However, I would argue that what occurs in some video game design and subsequent depictions goes beyond just cultural appropriation, which is to take something to use or consume from the original culture. Instead, games are trying to re-represent that culture. As discussed in Chapter 1, those from outside are trying to encapsulate a bound entity or the essence of a culture from surface representations they see in media or through limited knowledge, rather than constructing relational and dialogical understandings of the culture through their own experiences (Rogers, 2006). The larger issue at play here is not necessarily one of partaking in and engaging with the culture, but rather one of education and how we represent that culture, especially in the public arena. However, in some disciplines, such as teaching, we may still need to engage with and even represent the culture despite the dangers of misrepresentation.

In the education discipline, there are similar issues and dilemmas around teaching content about different cultures and communities with only materials. For example, Australian teachers are required to teach students about Indigenous Australia as a part of the curriculum and the cross-curriculum priorities (Australian Curriculum Assessment and Reporting Authority, 2022). However, if teachers teach using only essentialised understandings of cultures and communities learned from textbooks, it can create misrepresentations in the minds of students. In some cases, using only textbooks to teach about Indigenous Australians and their cultures may create the impression that their cultures are static and their communities trapped in the past. Some students may even believe Indigenous Australians no longer exist, or if they do, it is only in extremely remote communities. To further compound the problem, most teachers may not have any in-depth experience with Indigenous communities themselves.

However, teachers still need to teach about Australia's Indigenous culture and history as a part of their curriculum. This requirement, while not perfect, is important as not teaching about Indigenous Australia is to exclude the culture and deny the existence or historical significance of the people. Exempting the history in many cases may be even more detrimental and feed into myths such as Terra Nullius and the denial of a meaningful presence of Indigenous people on a land. In game design, we might face similar dilemmas. As not including a community or culture where they should be reflected can be even more problematic than potentially basic or generic representations. This dilemma is also an issue of representation, as a representation can be inclusive as well as exclusive depending on the image of the world being presented to the audience. Therefore, avoiding depicting cultures and communities altogether is not always a solution and can present a different set of issues around representation.

Whether these representations are appropriate may depend on your situation, and you will need to make these ethical and epistemological decisions as a game designer. A game with a significant section of the game dedicated to reflecting a specific culture should involve community participation, designer immersion in the culture and engagement in rigorous research. However, there may be cases where culture forms only a small part of the game or the designers are unable to engage the community in full. In these situations, designers may need to depict the culture through mostly rigorous research, as non-depictions could be more harmful in some instances (e.g. non-depictions of Indigenous Australia feed into the myth of Terra Nullius). However, these situations will need to be assessed on their own merits, and if you do proceed, realise your game will not carry the same cultural depth as those who hold the experience and involvement of those from the community. In some cases, you may very well be creating a Dogai that is not a true reflection of the culture or community. Nevertheless, these are ethical decisions for you to reflect on and make as a designer.

Torres Strait language – Torres Strait Creole

Torres Strait Creole is a contemporary dialect mostly derived from English. Torres Strait Creole is becoming more common and the predominant language in the Torres Straits. Torres Strait Creole is a mix of Island languages, English and languages from other cultures due to proximity or immigration. The following are some Torres Strait Creole words and their origins:

Torres Strait Creole words:

- Wichway – How are you?
- Sameway – I am good.
- Yumi (you and me) – Us.
- Yawo – Goodbye.
- Wa – Yes.
- Nor – No.
- Pasin – fashion (in the way of good fashion or island fashion).
- Sabe – to know such as me no sabe (I don't know). Perhaps derived from Spanish.

Shared Indonesian words in Creole:

- Makan – To eat or food.
- Suma Suma – Same to you.
- Doodoo – Sit.
- Terima kasih (bunya) – Thank you (very much).

Shared Papua New Guinea word in Creole:

- Kaikai – To eat or food.

Shared Japanese word in Creole:

- Namas (or Namasu) – Pickled fish.

Shared Filipino word in Creole

- Dinuguan – Pork cooked in pig's blood.

In designing a cultural game ethically with the community, it is likely you will see ethical dimensions of the culture represented in the game itself. For example, in the game *Pamali: Indonesian Folklore Horror* (StoryTale Studios, 2018), players must typically navigate and interact with different day-to-day objects and cultural artefacts in the environment to progress through the game. These interactions can include cleaning, moving or removing an object, which can affect how the spiritual being in-game acts towards the player. These actions may break taboos (Setyawati et al., 2021), which can anger the spirit or, in some cases, ward off the ghostly antagonist of the game. Here, protocols are embedded into decision-making and your decisions have cultural impacts, which are in a way ethical decisions about how you also respect and engage with the culture. These decisions affect how you progress through the game to various endings.

Pamali's core mechanic of taboos forms the entire high-level gameplay and is very likely a reflection of the ethical game design processes of the development team. The game system is an ethical object that is governed by the rules of the game and players are ethical beings who react to the game in ethical ways (Sicart, 2009). The game's ethical systems of choosing to break or obey certain taboos are reflections of the game development team's intimate knowledge of Indonesian stories and their connections to the community. As a player, you are ethically engaging with the game by choosing whether or not to break cultural taboos and the consequences of those actions. In this way, the ethics of a culturally centred game design process have reflected the ethics of the game systems. In games designed by Elizabeth LaPensée, we can also see how the ethics of a community inform game systems in games such as *Honour Water* (Pinnguaq, 2016) and *Thunderbird Strike* (LaPensée, 2017). In both *Honour Water* and *Thunderbird Strike*, the player cannot lose the game, which was a design decision informed by input from Elders so as not to shame the player (LaPensée, 2020; LaPensée et al., 2018). A similar process occurred with TSVR, the ethical system of consideration of cultural protocols for the Tombstone Opening and your obligation to contribute and work with the rest of your community was fundamental to the game's premise and storyline. These are reflections of the ethics of the community that filter into the game design and are represented in the game system itself.

Part of this ethical engagement with the game is also the player's reflection on the journey or choices in-game. In this way, the game mechanics help players engage with and reflect on different ethical models of behaviour across different cultures and communities (McDaniel & Fiore, 2010). In contrast, Sicart (2009) points out that game moral systems such as *Star Wars: Knight of the Old Republic* (BioWare, 2003) and *Fable* (Big Blue Box Studios, 2004) allow the player to make ethical choices that affect the world with a clear "good" and "evil" understanding of the world. However, the moral choices in these games are strategies that are measured and evaluated by the game's system and not by moral choices that the player reflects on themselves. Similarly, in culturally centred games, these moral systems are not necessarily posed as strategies to be exploited, but rather as a reflection of a world view and a way of life to be respected in their own contexts.

Monetisation and the benefit that a developed cultural product might produce is another ethical issue in the game development process. In some cases, there may be no reciprocity, no giving back or even an acknowledgment of the communities depicted in games, which is a practice that can be seen as a core value to many cultures (Brayboy et al., 2012). Monetisation and how profits are generated from the game are important considerations and are of particular note if the communities depicted in the game do not benefit from their cultural representation (Church, 2022). In these cases, culture may only be seen as something to be taken and then exposed to a home audience for compensation without any payment to or acknowledgment of the home community (Rogers, 2006). Commodification of the culture can change the context of the original meaning and might be subject to market influences rather than what the original intent of the cultural practice is (Rogers, 2006). This issue might explain why certain aspects of the culture are accentuated to play into audience expectations. Therefore, when engaging with a community, monetary benefit as well as reciprocity and giving back are important aspects to consider.

The ethical domain is an important consideration in the design and overall development of games that represent other cultures. There are ethical decisions about how to include or represent communities and cultures in-game and it is important to represent communities in appropriate and thoughtful ways. Even if well intentioned, not depicting a community or culture, especially where it clearly should be depicted, can present issues in itself (e.g. Indigenous Australia and Terra Nullius). In some ways, it is about what is not depicted as much as what is depicted in-game. However, these are ethical and situational decisions for the designers to make. Ethics also manifests in the game design in how mechanics and game systems represent ethical systems of thought within a culture. *Pamali (StoryTale Studios, 2018)*, *Honour Water (Pinnguaq, 2016)* and *Thunderbird Strike (LaPensée, 2017)* represent ethical cultural understandings of the world, which are the mechanics, limitations and overall game systems. Monetisation also forms a part of ethical considerations and links into community considerations around compensating for those cultures we are benefiting from, especially when profits are made from such in-game representations.

Conclusion

In summary, cultural immersion can be used to support the designer's understanding of the culture and promote further experiences and relationships with the community. These relationships may evolve into reciprocal relationships that could extend beyond the project itself. Cultural immersion can allow learning through different avenues beyond cognition, such as through affect as well as pedagogies related to the Country/Place of the community. Cultural immersion can also be further supported through rigorous research with different materials. Rigorous research can help us consider the kinds of materials (e.g. better to use community-authored or supported materials) that we can use to build our game worlds. Rigorous research and the examination and use of different materials also provide designers with a theoretical understanding to the stories and knowledge shared by communities. Rigorous research can also be used to provide context for the cultural immersion experiences that the designers may undertake. Game designers will also need to consider and make ethical judgments and decisions about the process of reflecting cultures in-game, the representation of cultural ethics systems in-game and the handling of monetary compensation for communities where applicable. I urge designers to be thoughtful and ethical about the way they include and depict cultures in-game and that they engage in a process of reciprocity with those communities where possible.

Cultural immersion and rigorous research serve as valuable support mechanisms to aid in the construction of cultural game worlds. These approaches also provide better cultural understanding and knowledge construction for the designers building those game worlds. However, the most valuable and preferred method to integrate culture into the game is via community participation, with the community's direct input into the game design and the resulting game product. Yet, all three aspects of community participation, cultural immersion and rigorous research can be triangulated to support each other. This combined approach provides a strong foundation on which to centre your game development project. This multitiered strategy can introduce several avenues to embed cultural understandings into the design process. The resulting practice produces more meaningful gaming outputs that can help counter cultural misrepresentations and embed deep culture into video games.

References

Arya, R. (2021). Cultural appropriation: What it is and why it matters? *Sociology Compass*, *15*(10), e12923.

Australian Curriculum Assessment and Reporting Authority. (2022). *Australian Curriculum*. https://www.australiancurriculum.edu.au/

Bhardwaj, S. M. (1983). *Hindu places of pilgrimage in India: A study in cultural geography* (Vol. 14). University of California Press.

Big Blue Box Studios. (2004). *Fable* [video game]. Microsoft Game Studios.

BioWare. (2003). *Star wars: Knights of the old republic* [video game]. LucasArts.

Brayboy, B. M., Gough, H. R., Leonard, B., Roehl, R., & Solyom, J. A. (2012). Reclaiming scholarship: Critical indigenous research methodologies. In S. D. Lapan, M. L. T. Quartoli, & F. J. Riemer (Eds.), Qualitative research: An introduction to methods and designs (pp. 423–450). Jossey-Bass.

Burgess, C. (2019). Beyond cultural competence: Transforming teacher professional learning through Aboriginal community-controlled cultural immersion. *Critical Studies in Education*, *60*(4), 477–495.

Church, B. (2022). *Computer game design: A code of ethics*. Proceedings of the Wellington Faculty of Engineering Ethics and Sustainability Symposium. https://doi.org/10.26686/wfeess.vi.7641

Dewey, J. (1986). Experience and education. *The Educational Forum*, *50*(3), 241–252. https://doi.org/10.1080/00131728609335764

Doerr, N. M. (2013). Do 'global citizens' need the parochial cultural other? Discourse of immersion in study abroad and learning-by-doing. *Compare: A Journal of Comparative and International Education*, *43*(2), 224–243.

Eck, D. L. (2012). *India: A sacred geography*. Harmony.

Gainsford, A., & Robertson, S. (2019). Yarning shares knowledge: Wiradyuri storytelling, cultural immersion and video reflection. *The Law Teacher*, *53*(4), 500–512.

Gallagher, P., Mckinlay, E., Pullon, S., & McHugh, P. (2019). Student perceptions of cultural immersion during an interprofessional programme. *Journal of Interprofessional Care*, *33*(2), 264–266.

Gela, A. A. (1993). *Gelam the man from Moa: A legend of the people of the Torres Strait Islands*. Magabala Books.

Harrison, N., & Clarke, I. (2022). The impossibility of keeping history in the past: Working beyond cognitive science to locate historical significance in the stolen generations. *Asia-Pacific Journal of Teacher Education*, 1–15. https://doi.org/10.1080/13598 66X.2022.2151415

Harrison, N., & Skrebneva, I. (2020). Country as pedagogical: Enacting an Australian foundation for culturally responsive pedagogy. *Journal of Curriculum Studies*, *52*(1), 15–26.

LaPensée, E. (2017). *Thunderbird strike* [video game].

LaPensée, E. (2020). SPEAR: A framework for Indigenous cultural games. *ANTARES: Letras e Humanidades*, *12*(28), 4–22.

LaPensée, E., Day, S. M., & Jaakola, L. (2018). Honour water: Gameplay as a pathway to Anishinaabeg water teachings. *Decolonization: Indigeneity, Education & Society*, *7*(1), 115–130.

McDaniel, R., & Fiore, S. M. (2010). Applied ethics game design: Some practical guidelines. In *Ethics and game design: Teaching values through play* (pp. 236–254). IGI Global.

Pinnguaq. (2016). *Honour water* [video game]. https://apps.apple.com/app/id1146954514

Pope-Davis, D. B., Breaux, C., & Liu, W. M. (1997). A multicultural immersion experience: Filling a void in multicultural training. In D. B. Pope-Davis & H. L. K. Coleman (Eds.), Multicultural counseling competencies: Assessment, education and training, and supervision (pp. 227–241). Sage Publications, Inc.

Queensland Studies Authority. (2007). *Selecting and evaluating resources*. Brisbane. https://www.qcaa.qld.edu.au/downloads/approach2/indigenous_g008_0712.pdf

Rey, J., & Harrison, N. (2018). Sydney as an Indigenous place: "Goanna walking" brings people together. *AlterNative: An International Journal of Indigenous Peoples*, *14*(1), 81–89.

Rogers, R. A. (2006). From cultural exchange to transculturation: A review and reconceptualization of cultural appropriation. *Communication Theory*, *16*(4), 474–503.

Said, E. (1978). *Orientalism*. Routledge.

Setyawati, D. D. A., Retnowati, T. H., & Nugraha, W. M. (2021). A *Hyperreality Study on the Game Pamali: The White Lady (2018)*. 4th International Conference on Arts and Arts Education (ICAAE 2020). https://doi.org/10.2991/assehr.k.210602.053

Sicart, M. (2009). *The ethics of computer games*. MIT press.

Singh, R. P. (2020). Sacrality and waterfront sacred places in India: Myths and the making of place. In *Sacred Waters* (pp. 80–94). Routledge.

StoryTale Studios. (2018). *Pamali: Indonesian folklore horror* [video game]. StoryTale Studios and Maple Whispering Limited.

Tan, C. (2012). Deep culture matters: Multiracialism in Singapore schools. *International Journal of Educational Reform*, *21*(1), 24–38.

Thibeault, D. (2019). Understanding Indigenous culture through service learning and cultural immersion. *Journal of Social Work Education*, *55*(3), 476–488.

7 Designing to produce deep representations

The main problem addressed by this book has been the issue of misrepresentation of cultures and communities within video games, which often results from the game design process. Many cultures are depicted in video games, and in some cases, those games were created by designers not from those communities. These in-game representations can often be flawed and vary from clumsy depictions to extremely prejudiced representations to representations that homogenise several cultures into one (e.g. Native American nations) to non-depictions (omission or near absence of community) with many other forms of misrepresentation. This issue can be viewed through the frameworks of the cultural palm and the Dogai. I propose a continuum from the surface-level culture simulacrum, which is the Dogai, to the deeper culture, which is reflected in the Torres Strait cultural palm. Games that only represent the aesthetics and shallow understandings of the culture shift towards Dogaism, which is recognised as shallow by the community. On the other hand, games that draw from the deeper aspects of the culture to represent communities' in-game align closer with the cultural palm. The palm also represents shifts in culture and how culturally focused games can still be representative of deep culture while not being an exact replication of the original cultural product. The issue here is not that the culture is being reproduced in a different form or even depicted in a different way, but rather the process under which that game was created, how the game exists in relation to the actual culture and community and to what extent the game is viewed outwardly as a representation of the culture and its people.

In response to these challenges, I have focused on the game design process for Torres Strait Virtual Reality (TSVR) to explore how culture was centred and embedded into the game through various design decisions and considerations. From this exploration, I have suggested specific game design decisions such as centring your game premise around deep cultural practices, embedding cultural detail wherever practicable to avoid homogenisation and involving the community from the beginning. However, as an overarching high-level response, I propose that embedding culture into game design is best achieved through a three-tiered approach of community participation, cultural immersion of the designers and

DOI: 10.1201/9781003276289-10

rigorous research into the culture. Community participation can range from having team members from the community in your game development team to engaging a cultural expert to involving the community in the quality assurance and playtest processes. In these cases, those with lived experiences and intimate connections to the culture are centrally involved and help shape the game from their perspective. In addition to community participation, I also recommend that the game designers themselves undergo cultural immersion and, where possible, form a reciprocal relationship with the community. Designers can further supplement community participation and their own cultural immersion with rigorous research about the culture and community in question. Rigorous research with various materials can be used to gain a theoretical understanding to compare and contrast with input from the community as well as the designers' own experiences. However, rigorous research also requires us to be thoughtful about the materials that we use when building game worlds. Collectively, I anticipate that these design approaches can help inform designers about how to thoughtfully incorporate cultural representations into their game as well as provide opportunities for designers to form their own deeper connection with the culture and community.

If there was one point to take away from the book, I would urge those building game worlds to consider how culture fits into those worlds and how we can genuinely and thoughtfully represent those cultures in all their vibrancy. This book is not intended for you to avoid inserting culture into your game altogether, but to consider following a process of engaging with the community and reflecting on how to depict deeper aspects of culture in-game. If we can bring deep culture into the game world, we can truly benefit from the interesting cultural stories, knowledge and practices that will help bring those game worlds to life in their full complexity. This cultural profundity may not be possible without deep culture and community support. By following a culturally centred approach with community, not only would those from outside your community engage with the culture in-game in a genuine way, but also the communities that your game reflects could also enjoy the game and see themselves in the game. Therefore, community integration into game design and embedding deep representations of culture in games remain of paramount importance.

Integrating culture into video games and game design should be performed in a thoughtful way, and as a best practice, the process should involve community participation. However, ultimately, game designers will have to make ethical decisions based on their own time, resources and circumstances of the project. Even in partnership with the community or being from the community yourself, you still may not satisfy everyone in depicting culture in-game. Yet, crucially, we should be working towards involving those with cultural and community experiences where possible and striving to resolve our own limited understandings of the culture, so that we are self-reflexive and those limited understandings do not become the representative face of the culture and the community in games.

Torres Strait story – Pontianak

Pontianak is a female spirit who preys on young men at night. She is said to live in a frangipani tree, although in other stories she lives in a banyan tree or banana tree. Her story is thought to have originated in Indonesia and the wider Malay Archipelago. Pontianak does not feature in TSVR, but is still an important story character for some Islander people.

Cultural lens, representation and self-reflection

I have suggested several measures to address cultural biases and promote better cultural forms of representation through the designer's work. However, as individuals, the representations that we construct in our minds will always be, to some degree, through our own cultural lens. We are always making sense of our new cultural experiences in relation to our previous understandings and biases, and our experiences of other cultures will be our own cultural experience of another culture (e.g. a outsider does not have an Indonesian experience; instead, they have a foreigner's experience of Indonesia). When we design and produce media, how the audience interprets and understands the culture in the media will be through their own cultural lens. As designers, we can set soft boundaries within which the player can make sense of the culture in-game; however, there is still an interpretation and reshaping of the experience by the player (Calleja, 2013). In this way, we cannot directly control the audience and what they choose to hear or see in our own cultural representations. Indeed, this individual interpretation through processes and interactions is a core part of engagement with games, that is, where players make their own choices in-game, see the consequences, reflect on their actions and construct knowledge in their own minds from this process. Much of this process is completely removed from the game. Therefore, it is hard to control reinterpretations of the culture within games.

As designers, we are also dealing with the epistemological issue of constructing knowledge of the cultures and communities in-game according to our own terms. However, as designers, the recognition that we are understanding other cultures through our own cultural lens is a strong position to start from in our design process. Here, acknowledgement and awareness of the issue as well as reflecting on it is a sound practice to help avoid misrepresentations and to promote self-reflection of our own cultural biases. I suggest community participation, cultural immersion and rigorous research as measures to promote better and deeper cultural representations in the design and output. Built into these measures is also the practice for the designers themselves to better engage with the culture through their own experiences with it. These measures do not guarantee that the designer will have a clear cognition of the culture in the same way those from the culture understand it. However, these measures do allow us as designers to increase our chances of better understanding the culture in its deeper form. We are then, in conjunction with the community, better able to represent this deep culture in our game and communicate deeper representations to the audience. Hopefully, with these more genuine and deeper representations, we can encourage deeper cultural representations in the mind of the audience that better reflect the community's representation of themselves. Collectively, the measures of community participation, cultural immersion and rigorous research can be triangulated to enhance the individual methods to better inform and shape the game design process.

Triangulation of methods, knowledge and perspectives to embed culture into game design

In my suggested approach to embedding culture into game design, designers should utilise multiple methods to support the game design process, which can be combined in an approach called triangulation. In research, triangulation is the combination of different data, investigators or methodical approaches within the same study to support, confirm and enhance the conclusion (Thurmond, 2001). It is argued that by using multiple investigators, sources and methods in research, the researchers can develop a comprehensive understanding of a phenomenon (Carter et al., 2014). Triangulation is also considered a process of testing the credibility (trustworthiness) and validity (accuracy) of the data, investigators and methods through the convergence of information from different sources (Carter et al., 2014). This approach can help find the credibility and validity of what is being investigated (Noble & Heale, 2019). Credibility and validity have limited strength in this context, as culture and experience can be highly subjective and vary between community members and information sources. However, it is valuable for comparing and contrasting the input from different community members, sources of information and so on. Triangulation can be applied on multiple levels within the project in regards to the method for embedding culture, who we engage in the game design process and the sources of information we use to construct our game world.

First, we can triangulate different types of information through community participation, cultural immersion and rigorous research to better embed culture into game design. Similar to the convergence of data in research, we can see the convergence of different cultural stories and knowledge throughout the process. These convergences are compared and contrasted with each other to support their validity, which then feeds into the game design and is then communicated through different game processes. For example, several accounts of the same cultural story from different sources may provide varying details, but you may find there are essential themes or morals that remain consistent through all of the accounts.

Second, we can see the convergence of investigators in a research project, there are convergences of information from different community members, each of whom has a different perspective. One perspective from the community might provide insight into the culture that other sources may not provide. Each perspective brings their own experiences and how these have shaped their understanding of culture. These convergences are also representative of the diversity of community participation through the game design process and the output. These convergences can reflect the process of engaging a wealth of different community perspectives and even smaller groups within a community. For example, different members of the community may explain the same piece of knowledge in different ways and have different perspectives afforded by their position (e.g. an Elder or different culture-related roles) in the community. In some cases, different parts of the community share the same story with varying details.

Third, we can also see the convergence of different methodologies. We can see there are different approaches from engagement with the community to cultural immersion to rigorous research. Each of these understandings provides different insights into culture; some are likely deeper such as community participation but others provide the designer with their own experiential understanding or cultural knowledge from authored materials from the community. For example, feedback about a cultural practice from the community will make more sense through our own cultural immersion experiences than perhaps just having read about the culture in a book. Each of these methods adds another layer of understanding to enrich a more holistic, culturally centred approach to design.

Through different approaches such as community participation, cultural immersion and rigorous research, we are evaluating, balancing and triangulating different understandings to produce a more culturally sound game design process and, hopefully, a fuller cultural representation embedded into the game itself. While these efforts are no guarantee that in-game cultural depictions will not face criticism from the community, they do mean we have a better chance at deeper and more respectful cultural representations in-game. We can then say that thorough and culturally centred processes were put in place to best ensure deeper and more thoughtful cultural depictions in-game. See Figure 7.1 for a visualisation of how the different approaches are triangulated.

Benefits of a thoughtful approach to cultural representations and finding the balance

In game development, designers face limitations to resources, time and who they can recruit into the game development team. The project team will clearly need to balance their time, resources and team members. However, in regards to community participation, cultural immersion and rigorous research, these practices typically involve small costs and investments that are outweighed by the benefits. Through investments in these commitments, from a public relations perspective, designers have undertaken a process to work towards being culturally sound with participation from those in the community. The game will likely face less or no criticism from the community, which would have a legitimate right to criticise the game if they were not involved. However, from a game design perspective, these different practices bring more community voices into the game, adding a layer of cultural depth. Designers will likely have far more

TRIANGULATION OF EMBEDDING CULTURE INTO GAME DESIGN

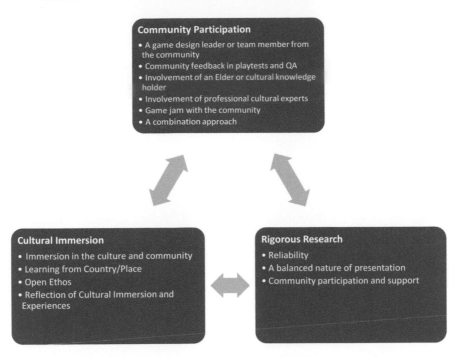

Figure 7.1 Triangulation of embedding culture into game design. Each approach supports the other, with community participation validating, contrasting, confirming and providing context to the designers own cultural immersion experiences and understandings learned through various materials. Cultural immersion experiences of the designers allow them to begin the process of building reciprocal relationships with the community and helping understand the culture, albeit through their own cultural lens. Rigorous research provides a theoretical framework to make sense of the community's remarks and experiences and the cultural immersion experiences of the designer [graphical diagram].

materials for their story and game premise earlier on in the game development process. This approach can help shape a more genuine cultural story and build a game world steeped in culture from the ground up. A thoughtful approach to involving the community in the design process can produce sound ethical and epistemological cultural representations in the game. These representations can prompt a more respectful and faithful construction of the culture in the minds of the audience. In this way, designers should aim to integrate community participation early on to prevent any issues later on and integrate cultural perspectives, stories and knowledge into the foundation of the game.

While there is a balance between the time, resources and staff allocated to the project in order to properly represent culture in-game, I would say the benefits of a thoughtful approach to cultural representations in-game outweigh the small cost to

CULTURAL APPROACH AND PRACTICAL INVESTMENT BALANCE

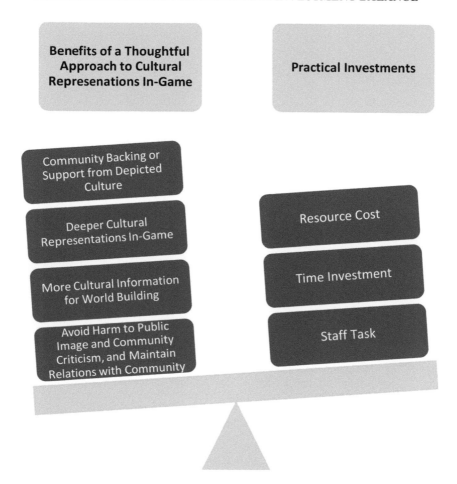

Benefits of a Thoughtful Approach to Cultural Represenations In-Game

Practical Investments

Community Backing or Support from Depicted Culture

Deeper Cultural Representations In-Game

Resource Cost

More Cultural Information for World Building

Time Investment

Avoid Harm to Public Image and Community Criticism, and Maintain Relations with Community

Staff Task

Figure 7.2 Having measures in place to build better cultural representations could have sig-nificant benefits compared with relatively small investments [graphical diagram].

time, resources and staff. The scales tilt towards having measures around cultural representation fulfilled at least to some degree. See Figure 7.2 to view the balance between the considerations. Even a small investment of time, resources and staff could add real value to the game and the project overall as well as the designer's reputation. This is particularly the case for larger companies and organisations. A thoughtful approach to cultural representation in the game and the design process could offer the following benefits:

- Backing or support from the community represented in-game.
- Deep cultural representations in-game.
- More cultural information to build your game world with.

- Potentially avoid harm to the project team's public image, drawing criticism from the community and creating frosty relations with the community depicted in-game.

There are benefits to the entire enterprise on various levels. On a game design level, the designers benefit from more cultural information to build the game world. On a project level, the team can save face publicly and obtain support from the community in building their game. On an ethical and epistemological level, the designers are representing deep culture in-game and can be confident that measures were put in place to support a culturally centred approach to the game design process.

It should also be said that each gaming project will be different, and the way designers represent culture will differ. In some cases, designers may need to think about different ways to depict culture and how they can embed culture in the game design process. For example, the absence of models of people in TSVR meant culture and community were communicated primarily through narration and strategically developed assets such as sketches converted into constellations. Each game and the design challenges that you encounter will require different solutions and you will have to think about how these challenges can be resolved in respectful, ethical and epistemologically sound ways. Not all practices of embedding culture into the game will be easily achievable. For example, developing meaningful and long-standing relationships with the community. However, there still needs to be thoughtful efforts around the game design process and representations in the game. Even less involved ways, such as assessing the appropriateness of different materials to inform the game's story and world design, will still help enhance the process. Nonetheless, these decisions about cultural depictions in-game and embedding culture in the game design process will be ones that designers will need to make. It is about being thoughtful about how we represent cultures in-game and being considerate of the community.

Torres Strait animals and plant – Torres Strait Pigeon and Wongai tree

The Torres Strait/White Pigeon (or Gainau in KLY) and the Wongai tree are typically associated with the Torres Straits and often found in the region. The Torres Strait Pigeon can be recognised by its striking black and white plumage. The pigeons were also traditionally hunted for their meat. The Gainau are present in traditional stories from the Torres Strait. The Wongai tree typically produces small fruits once a year. The Wongai or Torres Strait plums are quite sweet and sticky fruits, similar to those of dates. They say once you eat a Torres Strait plum, you will always come back to the Torres Straits. See Figure 7.3 for photographs of the Wongai tree and plum, and Figure 7.4 for a sketch of a Torres Strait Pigeon.

Figure 7.3 Wongai tree and fruit [photographs].

Figure 7.4 Torres Strait Pigeon [sketch]. Sketch by Gehamat Loban.

Process over outcome

Throughout the book, I have discussed the importance of representation and how many in-game representations of various communities are misrepresentations. These cultural representations in-game are the output of the process of constructing them. Thus, the process determines the output. In this way, I would argue that the process is more important than the output. Through the framework of the cultural palm and the Dogai, we can see process and output, but from polar opposite perspectives. The Dogai is a weak process with an outcome that could look sound but is not internally coherent, and this incoherence is especially recognised by those from the community. The cultural palm is the opposite. The palm requires thoughtful engagement with the process and for the creator to draw from longstanding traditions, beliefs, customs, values and cultural practices and understandings to inform the process. The strong foundation of the process provides the basis for a strong culturally centred outcome. The end outcome may not always look exactly like the previous outcome of deep culture, but if drawing from deep culture, the output still comes from a deep place and is typically accepted by the community.

The importance of process is also highlighted in the engagement with the community and community organisations. As an opposite to the importance of quick and time-effective decisions in certain organisations (e.g. some corporations), many community organisations emphasise the process of wide engagement and community consensus as the most important aspect. In some community organisations, the process of coming together, talking, deliberating and reaching an agreement is often at the heart of the practice. These are community-centred processes that help maintain relations within the community. Moreover, the decisions that come from these processes have undergone rigorous community processes and are highly consensual. Indeed, some of these practices of community consensus are an important part of and an obligation for social relations, kinship groups and families.

The Critical Indigenous Research Methodologies (CIRM) exemplifies a community-centred approach and utilises core elements of relationality, responsibility, respect and reciprocity (Brayboy et al., 2012). These elements are all centred around the practice of community and social engagement as a form of research and knowledge production. CIRM and similar frameworks are responses to past approaches to knowledge construction where knowledge was only an end product. These past approaches may have had little regard for the process by which that knowledge is created and the ethics surrounding its creation. Therefore, I see CIRM and similar frameworks as efforts to acknowledge a different way to formulate knowledge centred around the community and consensual practice.

In some cases, the primary aim of the process is not to create a tangible output, say in the form of a game product. Instead, it is the social process of working with the community, forming relationships and helping them in the representation of their own culture that is the primary goal. This approach could be a way of upskilling the community, so they have a better capacity to represent themselves using digital tools. These processes could also allow the community to break into a new digital space where they may not have had the opportunity to represent themselves.

For example, the Sámi community worked with developers to learn and help embody cultural knowledge through game jams (Laiti, 2021). The representation at the end of the process is a cultural world view and the culmination of an epistemological process of constructing cultural knowledge in a game form. Similar to productive failures, learning, rather than the tangible end product, is the important process (Kapur, 2008). The end outcome is the process of learning, working together on a cultural product and building with those relationship inside and outside of the community. At the end of the process, all that is left is representation.

Game designing with confidence to produce impactful gaming outputs

Game designers may choose to avoid the inclusion of some cultures in their game design due to a sense of apprehension about not getting it right or that there is too much angst and sensitivity around the inclusion of cultures. On the contrary, rather than dwell on these issues, designers should feel confident to represent cultures and communities in-game after having followed a culturally centred and epistemologically and ethically sound game design process. Designers can be assured that by involving the community and giving them a central position in shaping the project, the gaming product will be strongly shaped by the community and very likely representative of deep culture. Furthermore, by participating in the community and culturally immersing themselves, designers become familiar with the culture and can get a better sense of community perspectives in the project and from other community-authored materials. From this basis, designers can strongly compare and contrast their own cultural experiences with those from the community and other sources to better understand the culture.

Designers can say they are confident in their representation as they have followed a multitiered process and put several measures in place to ensure a level of engagement from the community and use of deep culture within the game design process. Designers can be self-assured they have worked in partnership with the community to produce a culturally sound product. In some cases, designers can say they have not only followed a culturally sound process, but that their products advocate for important issues for the community and may represent different cultural worldviews. Rather than merely meeting baseline expectations from the community, gaming outputs can transform into platforms to advocate for community issues and perspectives.

Book limitations and future practice and research

Having developed a game about the Torres Straits and being a Torres Strait Islander myself, my focus in this book has mostly been on Torres Strait culture, to a lesser extent other Indigenous cultures around the globe and very briefly other communities. As mentioned, there are already other projects that have their own cultural game design approaches such as *When Rivers Were Trails* (The Indian Land Tenure Foundation, 2019) and *Thunderbird Strike* (LaPensée, 2017), which were developed by Elizabeth LaPensée in conjunction with her community. In LaPensée's (2020) approach to game design, she implements the SPEAR model, where the Anishinaabe methodology called Biskaabiiyang forms the foundation of the model and centres community involvement. SPEAR advocates bringing community collaborations into centre focus, particularly early on in the project. In another example, Laiti (2021) discusses the digital árran, a theoretical framework based on a Sámi approach to education, which is a Sámi method for constructing and sharing knowledge. Digital árran came out of research involving game jams involving Sámi people. Other game-related projects such as the *Good Bag* mod by Ong et al. (2022) for *Beat Saber* (Beat Games, 2018) also provide insight into how cultural considerations and practices while working with the Chinese community to shape digital game-based outputs. While mods have limitations and can only be modified within a framework, they can still be used as a platform for cultural expression. Given the Torres Strait focus of this book, there are certainly other cultural game design approaches to explore. Indeed, future projects could examine how other cultures have been embedded into games. These projects will likely be from the perspectives of communities with their own approaches to embedding culture into game design and into their video games. However, there are still relatively few given how many video games depict different cultures. Future research could not only examine projects integrating culture into games built from scratch but also include other game-related practices such as modding.

In a professional game design setting, I anticipate these culturally centred approaches to game design would become more commonplace. These approaches to culture in games should be standard with games that focus on a specific culture or community that is deeply entrenched in a game story or setting. Games that have minor inclusions of a culture or community should still follow a thoughtful approach to bringing culture into their games. These approaches are not only for the benefit of the communities but also for providing deeper cultural representation to more vividly bring game worlds to life.

Conclusion

Culture has been represented in various mediums throughout history, and digital games are no exception. Shallow and even harmful depictions of cultures are not a new problem, with games also susceptible to this issue. In response to this challenge, I propose a culturally centred approach to game design with a combination of countermeasures, including community participation, cultural immersion and rigorous research. Through actively applying such measures, deep cultural knowledge and worldviews could be the foundation from which games can be built. Designers have the opportunity to create more thoughtful and fuller cultural representations in the mind of the audience. I have explored the design of TSVR as an exemplar of integrating deep culture into the game design process. Throughout the development of TSVR, culture remained at the centre of the process. Cultural considerations determined how the game was designed, the game's content and depictions and the different people involved in the game's development. I propose that game designers can also implement similar measures in their projects to work towards producing richer cultural representations and more culturally sound gaming experiences.

Perhaps more importantly than just having a culturally sound game, designers also have the opportunity to work with communities to produce digital media to draw attention to important community issues and promote differing perspectives. In this way, through game design and the production of video game outputs, games can act as platforms to advocate for issues and perspectives of the community in a real sense through complex and meaningful gaming worlds. Games can be shifted from being platforms that at times perpetuate or feed into stereotypes and cultural illiteracy and instead become a medium to promote community perspectives and act as social advocacy for the culture represented in-game.

TSVR was a digital representation of a way of life in the form of the cultural responsibilities of the Tombstone Opening. The player's navigation and engagement with the island world are the process of fulfilling those duties. TSVR promotes a cultural perspective on the way one handles the passing of someone in the community with in-game stories and knowledge intimately linked with the island setting. For myself, the cultural representations in-game are more than just a digital recreation or a plaything; they are a real representation of a cultural worldview and a cultural artefact that joins other cultural outputs produced from deep culture. For me, the game is a reflection of how the community sees the culture and it is a way of life for those in the culture.

References

Beat Games. (2018). *Beat saber* [video game].

Brayboy, B. M., Gough, H. R., Leonard, B., Roehl, R., & Solyom, J. A. (2012). Reclaiming scholarship: Critical indigenous research methodologies. In. S. D. Lapan, M. L. T. Quartoli, & F. J. Riemer (Eds.), *Qualitative research: An introduction to methods and designs* (pp. 423–450). Jossey-Bass.

Calleja, G. (2013). Narrative involvement in digital games.

Carter, N., Bryant-Lukosius, D., DiCenso, A., Blythe, J., & Neville, A. J. (2014). The use of triangulation in qualitative research. *Oncology Nursing Forum, 41*(5), 545–547. https://doi.org/10.1188/14.ONF.545-547

Kapur, M. (2008). Productive failure. *Cognition and Instruction, 26*(3), 379–424.

Laiti, O. (2021). *Old ways of knowing, new ways of playing—The potential of collaborative game design to empower Indigenous Sámi* [Dissertation thesis]. University of Lapland.

LaPensée, E. (2017). *Thunderbird strike* [video game].

LaPensée, E. (2020). SPEAR: A framework for Indigenous cultural games. *ANTARES: Letras e Humanidades, 12*(28), 4–22.

Noble, H., & Heale, R. (2019). Triangulation in research, with examples. *Evidence Based Nursing, 22*(3), 67–68. https://doi.org/10.1136/ebnurs-2019-103145

Ong, Y., Loban, R. D., & Parrila, R. K. (2022). The fight is the dance: Modding Chinese martial arts and culture into beat saber. *Journal of Games Criticism, 5*(A), X–X.

The Indian Land Tenure Foundation. (2019). *When rivers were trails* [video game].

Thurmond, V. A. (2001). The point of triangulation. *Journal of Nursing Scholarship, 33*(3), 253–258.

Epilogue

Caring for the tombstone site

Remarks from Gehamat Loban

Figure 7.5 Great Dato's gravesite with different objects and a glass of water [photograph]. Year: 2022.

As time goes on, we always look after the tombstone site, as the grave is now the home of the deceased. If we do not live on the island, a family member who lives there will look after the tombstone sites on behalf of the family. See Figure 7.5 for a photograph of Great Dato Tom's gravesite. When we visit the gravesite, we start by

DOI: 10.1201/9781003276289-11

talking to the deceased and cleaning the gravesite. We wash out the cup and saucer that may already be there and fill up the cup with fresh water. Some families fill the cups with different beverages. We can also place biscuits or other food at the site. If the deceased enjoyed smoking, we could light a cigarette for them. We also pour water on the sides, at the feet of the coping and over the tombstone. This process is not just for the gravesite of one person, but for many of the family members who are buried in the graveyard. So, we might be cleaning and leaving food and drinks for many deceased family members. We also leave plastic flowers at the grave to decorate the site. If previously placed flowers have deteriorated over time, we can replace them with new flowers. Once a year, we may repaint the gravesite if there are fences around the gravesite. We clean the gravesite and lay down new sand and shell grit. Just like a home, we have to maintain the gravesite and treat the site like a home.

Index